Saints of SCOTLAND

Edwin Sprott Towill

SAINT ANDREW PRESS
EDINBURGH

First published in 1978 by
SAINT ANDREW PRESS
121 George Street, Edinburgh EH2 4YN

This revised and enlarged edition
published in 1983

Reprinted 1994

Copyright © Edwin Sprott Towill

ISBN 0 7152 0678 8

British Library Cataloguing in Publication Data
A catalogue record for this book
is available from the National Library.

ISBN 0-7152-0678-8

Cover photograph by Paul Turner.
Cover design by Mark Blackadder.

Printed by Athenaeum Press Ltd, Newcastle upon Tyne.

Saints of
SCOTLAND

TO KATE

Without whose unfailing
assistance and understanding
this edition of 'my Saints'
could never have been
contemplated, let alone its
last pages completed

'I should like to know, God's dear Saint, what work you did or what virtue you manifested that pleased Christ so much . . . I have no doubt that you had some special quality in regard to which none was found like you, and it is that quality which I propose to investigate . . . Open the ear of my understanding that I may know what it was.'

Meditation to the Most Blessed Cuthbert by an unknown fourteenth-century monk of Farne, translated by a Benedictine nun of Stanbrook.

Contents

Preface

This book is not just about Scottish saints; its purpose is to provide concise notes on the many saints whose names are commemorated not only in our Scottish churches but in the titles of towns, villages, farms and ancient ruins, in natural features like hills, wells and rivers and in stories from local folk-lore and legend. Many of these were Scots men and women, others never set foot in the country. I have included saints from England, Ireland, Wales and the continent, as well as Biblical characters and angelic figures—they are included here because of their links with Scotland's history as well as her religion.

It is now exactly a century since Bishop A. P. Forbes of Brechin published his *Kalendars of Scottish Saints* and the time has obviously come for a more modern book on the same lines. The first edition of this book was selective rather than comprehensive and omitted a number of figures of some importance. This second edition, in a humble way, seeks to approach more nearly the pattern set by Forbes in including all saints who might legitimately claim some Scottish connection.

I hope that my notes may be of interest and help to our many visitors, to teachers and to the general reader. In addition to sharing the saints of the wider Church Catholic, Scotland's historic heritage from the days of the Celtic Church provides her own gallery of missionaries, to whom, although they passed no examination such as was applied later to candidates for beatification, we apply, *honoris causa*, the designation 'saint'.

Some of these figures of the Celtic period are so little known that information is hard to obtain. I have tried to provide not only what is known, but what is thought probable in their history. Other figures, like Ninian and Columba have been written up many times, but unfortunately (except in scholarly works and learned papers) most accounts have done little more than repeat the rumours and standard miracles lifted from the mediaeval legendary *vitae* without paying regard to the researches and criticisms of the scholars of the last half-century, during which great advances have been made in understanding this period of history. As far as seemed possible in the limited scope of these pages, I have tried to portray the scene as the student of the Celtic Church today sees it, not entirely robbing St Kentigern (Mungo) of his robin, nor St Ninian of his cave by the Solway, but setting the discoveries of the archaeologist and the historian beside the legendary stories.

I owe a great debt to many scholars, from Bishop Reeves down to the present day, whose theories and conclusions I have had to plunder, often without full acknowledgment, in such a concise book. In addition to the primary sources, the martyrologies, the mediaeval *vitae* and the dictionaries (such as Baring-Gould's), two writings have been of great assistance: the late J. M. Mackinlay's *Ancient Church Dedications in Scotland* and the late G. A. Frank Knight's *Archaeological Light on the Early Christianising of Scotland.* Both have to some extent been overtaken by more modern scholarship but they have not yet been superseded.

Edwin Sprott Towill
Edinburgh, 1982

What is a Saint?

The word 'saint' is not much used today—even by Christian people, for the impression it conveys is of far-away times and somewhat impossible, other-worldly, stained-glass figures.

In the early years of the Christian Church, however, this was not the case. The word 'saint' was almost synonymous with 'Christian'. When Paul writes 'to all the saints in Jesus Christ which are at Philippi', he simply means 'to the Philippi Christians'.

The Greek word was *hagios* which meant 'holy' but also retained its primary meaning of 'different' or 'separated'. Saints were holy people because they were Christians and they were different from and separated from the great body of unbelievers. A glance at any history of Roman and Greek society will illustrate why Christians were proud to be different not only in their faith and belief but in their morals and standards of life.

The word *hagios*, however, did not just mean 'different'; there was always the suggestion of 'difference upwards', towards holiness. In the Hebrew of the Old Testament we find the Jews used two words for this, both meaning 'difference upwards'.

But for the early Church to claim that 'saints' were different certainly did not mean that they were different from other Christians—they were separated from the non-Christians but not from one another. Later, however, as the numbers in the Church grew, the word became restricted to Christians who were outstandingly *hagios*. Those of particularly virtuous life or who had known faithfulness and constancy in times of persecution were felt to deserve this title and to stand alongside the 'witnesses' or martyrs who had died for the faith.

It was not until almost five centuries after the Crucifixion that the saints began to influence theology. From being regarded merely as grand examples of Christian life who should be remembered and honoured, they now became 'intercessors'. As they were surely in heaven we might pray, if not actually to them, through them to Christ and God. It was also felt that the virtue of the saints had built up a 'treasury of merit' in which other Christians might share through their prayers. Naturally, it was reasoned, the saints deserved something which was more than just respect. This was termed *douleia*, honour or veneration over against the worship we give to Christ and to God, which was termed in Greek *latreia*. Once it was accepted that the saints might intercede for us at the Throne of Grace, it became obvious that no mistake should be made between those who were and those who were not saints. What had previously been largely informal, a Christian being generally respected until he was given the title of saint, now had to be formalised.

The first known 'canonisation' was not till the year 993, although the word 'saint' had been used long before that date. The elaborate formal process by which the Western or Roman Church selects and canonises, after preliminary 'beatification', was not finalised for many years after that time. It consists, as is generally known, of a long probationary period, after which comes a type of trial with advocates pleading for and against the canonisation. One criterion, which is often questioned by non-Catholics, is the production of at least one miracle wrought through prayer to (or through) the candidate for sanctification.

The Roman Catholic Church is consistent in continuing to create new saints in modern times. The Anglican Church kept its kalendar of saints, as did the Scottish Episcopalians, with extra emphasis on figures from the Celtic Church, but none has been added since the Reformation, and probably no machinery now exists for sanctification. At the Reformation the reformed Churches, of which the major one is the Presbyterian, rejected the doctrine of the intercession of saints. They were especially sceptical about the many life-size images or statues, which seemed to them to be a focus for the superstitions of the ignorant. They also sensed danger lest the saints might be considered as mediators who would weaken the emphasis on the one Mediator, Jesus Christ. Not only was there no mention of individual saints in the Protestant liturgies, but remembrance of them on their festival days was forbidden. Although the parish churches of Scotland officially lost their 'patrons' in many places the name of the old saint continued in use as before.

One reason, perhaps, why Scotland did not much miss patrons and dedications was that before the Romanising of the Church of north Britain under Queen Margaret dedication of churches to saintly figures seems to have been unknown. The people simply spoke of the church at a certain place, or gave it the name of the pioneer missionary who founded it, and who had been responsible for the 'annat' or parent community. As a result the mediaeval Church found that many foundations bore the names of local saints, often quite obscure, of whose orthodoxy the Church authorities were by no means certain. It became usual to supplant the local saint by a more orthodox and universally known figure—an apostle, the Blessed Virgin or an archangel such as Michael. In some cases the name of the original saint survived, coupled to the new dedication—in this way Fearn Abbey became St Mary and St Ninian's. It will be seen that by the Middle Ages the word 'saint' was no longer restricted to deceased Churchmen but was prefixed to Mary the Virgin, and to archangels like Michael, while even sacred objects, like the Holy Rood, were considered possible patrons.

In course of time the very number of saints became a burden to the Church, and it included some mythical names. From time to time (and as recently as 1969), the Roman Catholic Church has carried out a purge of its lists.

We have pointed out that while veneration of saints was abolished by Presbyterians at the Reformation, in practice saints' names often remained in use in the relevant parishes. This practice has become accepted in recent years, although in choosing saints for new parishes the Presbyterians seem to have played for safety rather than variety, holding to one of the apostles so that we find a surfeit of St Matthews, Marks, Lukes and Johns, apparently chosen at random. Of the four, John the Evangelist has the closest historical connections with Scotland and its reformed tradition, through the Eastern liturgies upon which the reformers largely drew.

Dissenting groups of Presbyterians each had their own preferences when naming their chapels and they all avoided the mediaeval saints. In the eighteenth and nineteenth centuries it was fashionable to call the chapel after some prominent preacher in the denomination: so we find Chalmers' Memorial and similarly with Cairns, Candlish and other leaders. Some preferred simply to call their congregation by the street in which it was situated. The Reformed Presbyterian body, descendants of the Covenanting 'hillmen' invariably named their congregations after martyrs, and where we come across a Church of Scotland congregation today so named we can be sure it had its origins in the 'RP' body. Perhaps the most thoughtless and distasteful name for a united congregation was that of Holy Trinity, adopted not because of any affection for that theological concept but simply to indicate that three once separate churches were now in one.

The Church of Scotland has left it to the Scottish Episcopalians to select some of the attractive saints from the Celtic period for their new congregations. The Roman Catholic Church also has kept alive many good Scottish saints' names for its new churches.

One of the central beliefs of Christians has always been that of the Communion of Saints—the Church Militant on earth uniting with the Church Triumphant in glory, in a fellowship unbroken by death, to praise God through His Son, their Saviour. The saints are our witnesses to this faith. If we feel that to pray through them strengthens our petitions and intercessions, then we should do so; but if we desire that nothing should be interposed between ourselves and the Supreme Mediator, Christ, then we must still remember in thanksgiving the great Cloud of Witnesses who made our faith possible.

Kalendar of the saints' feasts or festivals. (These are usually the dates of their death.)

January
        7   Kentigerna
        8   Nathalan
        9   Fillan of Strathfillan
       13   Kentigern
            Kessog
       17   Antony
       19   Fillan of Strathfillan (alternative)
       20   Vigean
       26   Conan

February
        1   Bride or Bridget
        3   Ailred (alternative)
            Laurence
        4   Modan
        7   Ronan
       18   Colman
       23   Boisil
       24   Quivox
       28   Oswald

March
        1   David of Wales
        3   Ailred
        4   Adrian
        6   Baldred
       10   Kessog (alternative)

10 John Ogilvie
11 Constantine
17 Patrick
20 Cuthbert
30 Regulus (alternative)

April
2 Ebba the Second
16 Donan
Magnus
17 Donan (alternative)
18 Molios
21 Maelrubha
23 George
29 Brioc
Katherine of Siena
30 Brioc (alternative)
Katherine of Siena (alternative)

May
10 Gordian
16 Brendan
21 Godric
24 David I, King of Scotland

June
1 Ronan (alternative)
9 Baithene
Columba
16 Cyrus
22 Fillan of Loch Earn
23 Mochaoi
24 John the Baptist
29 Peter

July
1 Serf
7 Palladius
11 Drostan
18 Enoch
29 Olaf
31 Germanus

August
4 Moluag
10 Blane (alternative)
11 Blane
16 Roque
18 Marnock
22 Maelrubha (alternative)
25 Ebba of Northumbria
29 John the Baptist (alternative)
30 Ayle
31 Aidan

September
1 Giles
10 Finian
15 Mirren
16 Ninian
22 Llolan
23 Adamnan
28 Convall
29 Michael

October
8 Triduana
11 Kenneth
12 Edwin
  Wilfred
13 Comgan

17 Regulus
21 Fintan Munnu
25 Marnock (alternative)
31 Bega

November

3 Malachy
6 Leonard
8 Gerardine
9 Triduana (alternative)
11 Martin
12 Machar
13 Bryce
     Devenick
15 Fergus
16 Margaret
17 Hilda
22 Cecilia
27 Fergus (alternative)
30 Andrew

December

6 Nicholas
18 Monirus
22 Athernaise
27 John the Evangelist
29 Thomas

Saints with uncertain feast dates include—
Bonach, Christopher, Colm, Colmanella, Curitan, Duthac, Herbert, Katherine of Alexandria, Macdonald Maidens, Mary, Medan, Modwenna, Monan, Tarkin.

Adamnan whose name means 'Wee Adam', was born in Donegal about 627 of one of the branches of the Ui Neill clan. As such, he was directly related to Columba. He received a scholarly education, probably at Clonard, and entered the 'family of Columba' at Iona as a monk in the abbacy of Seghine. At the age of 55, he became the ninth abbot.

In 685, when Egfrith, the king of Northumbria, was defeated and slain at Nechtansmere (near Forfar) by Brude MacBile, the king of the Picts, Adamnan arranged for the body to be conveyed to Iona for burial. His permission for the funeral was the more charitable as Egfrith's fleet had taken a large number of Irish captives into slavery and one of Adamnan's tasks was to make the long journey to see Aldfrith, Egfrith's successor in Northumbria, to petition for their release. The second royal funeral was that of King Brude himself in 693 when Adamnan, tradition says, sat all night by the Rock of the Dead in vigil over the body. In the first light he thought he saw the body move and the eyes open, and he was about to revive it when a voice predicted evil if he persisted in doing so.

Adamnan attempted and succeeded in a most difficult literary task—writing a book about a place he had never visited. *De Locis Sanctis* is about the holy places of Palestine, and all Adamnan's information was obtained from a Gaulish bishop who spent a winter on Iona. His greater work is the remarkable biography of his predecessor Columba who had died just twenty-seven years before Adamnan was born. He divided this work into prophecies, miracles and visions, but the biographical material at the beginning and the end, and the many oblique references to people and their living conditions, make it a key reference work on the Iona of Columba's and, even more, of Adamnan's days.

As head of the 'parouchia Chaluimchille' Adamnan could not avoid involvement in the politics, especially the ecclesiastical politics, of his day. This entailed a considerable amount of travel, and it was probably on a visit to Northumbria in 688 that the Romanising party in the Church won him over to their side in the controversy which the synod of Whitby had opened up but by no means settled. He became enthusiastic about the efficiency, uniformity and seemliness of the reforms, and back on Iona he became dismayed that his monks could not be brought to share the same views. His life on Iona thenceforth seems to have been an unhappy one.

In 697 he crossed to Ireland to play a leading part in the synod at Birr which, in what are known as the Cain Adhannain or Adamnan's Law Code, passed several acts to raise the status of women, not by granting them equal status with men but by stressing the differences—stiffer penalties for assault of women, exemption from military duty and so on.

An early Irish legend suggests that Adamnan's resolve to push forward these reforms was due to an incident in his youth when, walking with his mother, he saw a woman dragging another along with a reaping hook transfixed through her breast. His mother made him promise to work for the protection of her sex from violence and war.

After this synod Adamnan probably remained

in Ireland for the final seven years of his life. The discord between himself and his Iona 'family' had become so acute that no other course was possible. With this cloud over him, he died in 704, aged about 78. His body was taken to Iona for burial.

In spite of his importance, the only surviving memorial to Adamnan in Iona is the name of a creek, Port Adhamhnain, just east of the pier. Formerly, there was also a Crois Adhamhnain. Around Scotland there are a large number of sites which bear his name in one form or another (there are over twenty variations of Adamnan's name). The following is a selection, bearing in mind (as always) that such a name is no guarantee of a visit from the saint himself— without further evidence it may only be the indication of a late mediaeval cultus.

At Crois Aon'ain on Sand Island, North Uist, is a carved cross on a boulder. Killeonan, in Kilkerran parish, Kintyre, had a chapel dedicated to Adamnan, and in Glen Urquhart, Abriachan had both a chapel and a croft in his name. Insch parish (Inverness) was in his patronage, as was Tannadice which has a hill called St Arnold's Seat. In Banffshire is Teunankirk, while Aboyne is also his and has the Skeulan Well. Glen Lyon has a tradition that the saint died there and was buried originally at Dull which had a Feill-Aonain (Adamnan's Fair). Beside the Bridge of Balgie is a mill and an island where he baptised converts. Finally, at Craigiannie there is a cross shaft erected where he prayed to avert plague from the glen.

Adamnan's festival day is 23 September.

G. A. F. Knight, *Archaeological Light on the Early Christianising of Scotland*, 1933
D. Pochin Mould, *The Irish Saints*, 1964

ADRIAN (there are many variations of his name, including Magirdle) was a later missionary of the Celtic Church, martyred on the Isle of May in the Firth of Forth near the end of the ninth century. Perhaps Adrian, said to have been a young disciple of Acca of Hexham, was involved in the fighting which accompanied the final downfall of Pictish power. The historian Skene has attempted to disentangle the strands of this obscure story which ends with the invasion of the Danes, their descent on the Isle of May and the martyrdom of Adrian and his followers in 875.

Adrian has been credited with some of the remarkable cave carvings found along the mainland shore opposite the island. At the opposite end of Fife, in that corner where Perthshire and Fife meet, we find a group of place-names reminding us of this unfortunate missionary. In Dron parish is Exmagirdle (ecclesia Magirdle) with a ruined chapel. At Abernethy stand two large crosses, one of which is known as Mugdrum Cross, probably named after Adrian, and along the estuary of the Tay at Flisk a group of stones is called St Muggin's Seat. So if his traditions have any historical substance it is to north Fife as well as to the Isle of May that we should look for traces of his work.

His festival is 4 March.

G. A. F. Knight, *Archaeological Light on the Early Christianising of Scotland*, 1933

AIDAN of Lindisfarne was the brightest star in the galaxy of Northumbrian saints but his orbit was by no means wholly English in the

modern sense, for in his day Lothian was an integral part of the kingdom of the Angles which stretched from Edinburgh to York. He carried the spirit and genius of Celtic Christianity as far south as Yorkshire and established on the island of Inis Medcoit, or Lindisfarne, a community in the east modelled on the pattern of the western Iona.

Had it not been for the defeat and death of Edwin, the first Northumbrian Christian king, Aidan would probably have lived and died a simple monk in the monastery of Iona. Among the lay brothers at that time there was a family of royal refugees, the princes and a princess of the Angles, who had fled there in 617 when Edwin had defeated their father, King Aethelfrith, to secure his throne. Oswald, one of the princes, was baptised a Christian, and when Edwin fell in battle at the hands of Cadwallen of Gwynedd, he seized the throne of Bernicia (the northern sector of Northumbria) and sent back to Iona for monks to re-evangelise his lands, which had fallen back to paganism on Edwin's death. This time it was not to be the Romanised form of Christianity from Canterbury, but the Celtic strain from the north. Aidan was not the first choice for the task. The abbot of Iona, Seghine, picked a monk called Corman who soon proved so unsuitable that the mission was closed down. King Oswald, however, was determined that it must succeed. Seghine called a conference of his monks at Iona and when suggestions were invited young Aidan spoke up: 'It seems to me, brother, that you were too hard on your ignorant listeners and should first have given them the milk of milder instruction and gradually instructed them in the Word of God.'

Aidan was then chosen to lead the mission and

proved to be the man called forth by the hour for a task which demanded just the talents he possessed. He had to work closely with his king, who spent much of his time at Bamburgh, his capital, which was also the mission headquarters. As is evident from the anecdotes in Bede, the paths of the two were constantly crossing, which is probably one reason why Aidan asked for possession of the nearby island of Lindisfarne, whither he transferred his community. He and the king maintained mutual respect for one another and as the king was a man of forceful personality it says a lot for the saint that he worked happily as second in command, turning away Oswald's wrath when he sensed that he had to insist on the Christian course being adopted. Aidan's own sincerity and sanctity were both obvious but he also possessed the organising ability necessary to run the community successfully, and by his own learning and appreciation of the arts, Lindisfarne came to excel the Celtic settlements in Alba (Scotland) in sculpture and lettering. The great Lindisfarne Gospels are the outstanding example of the latter.

Monasteries established as daughters of Lindisfarne included Melrose, Hexham, Whitby and Coldingham. Bede sums up Aidan's work in a passage worth quoting:

> He gave his clergy an inspiring example of self-discipline and continence, and the highest recommendation of his teaching to all was that he and his followers lived as they taught. He never sought or cared for any worldly possessions and loved to give away to the poor whatever he received from kings and wealthy folk. Whether in town or country he always travelled on foot unless compelled by necessity to ride, and whenever he met anyone, whether high or low, he stopped and spoke to them. If they were heathen he urged them to be baptised, and if they were Christians he strengthened their faith.

The partnership with Oswald ended with the king's death in 642. His brother Oswy succeeded him in Bernicia, the northern part, and a cousin, Oswin, in Deira, the southern. To both of these Aidan acted as friend and adviser. His friendship with King Oswin was particularly close. Bede recounts that Oswin was once much annoyed with the saint when he found that a valuable horse which he had given him had been handed away to a beggar with all its valuable harness. 'Have we not in the stables many other animals suitable for a beggar without giving him the one I had selected specially for you?' asked the king. Aidan replied, 'Is this foal of a mare more valuable than the Son of God?' Oswin fell to his knee in penitence.

In 651 Aidan died after being abbot of Lindisfarne for seventeen years. He died in the church he had founded at Bamburgh, in part a disappointed man because he had not managed to achieve peace between Oswy and Oswin, and the latter had been betrayed and murdered a few months before. The wooden beam against which the saint leant in his death agonies outside the church was kept and later, when a new church was built, it was taken inside, where it is shown today. The traditional spot where he died is still held in respect in the church and nearby, a modern stained-glass window shows the first meeting of Oswald and Aidan.

On Lindisfarne today there is no trace of the early Celtic monastery. Its site may be that of the later parish church or that of the later mediaeval abbey, but local tradition believes it to be on the Heugh, a rocky height showing traces of ancient ruins. The well-known sculptor, Kathleen Parbury, who herself lived on the island for several years, carved the great impressive statue of St

Aidan which looks over to the Heugh, with the parish church on its right and the abbey ruins to the left.

The number of churches we find dedicated to Aidan in the Breadalbane district has caused some scholars to suggest that while Oswald was in exile in Iona the saint was away evangelising in Alba. Inchadney in Glen Lyon was once Inchaidan, as also was the ancient name of Kenmore. An island in Loch Tay was Eilean Aidan. In Angus at Menmuir was a chapel to the saint. Aidan's symbol is a torch, probably because when the pagan king Penda was burning Bamburgh it was said that the flames were averted when the wind changed at the saint's prayers.

His festival is 31 August, and at that day the Irish martyrologies note him as 'Aidan, the bright sun of Innis Medcoit'.

H. Mayr-Harting, *The Coming of Christianity*, 1972
K. Parbury, *The Saints of Lindisfarne*, 1970

ᴀɪꞁʀᴇᴅ was born in 1109, the son of a married priest of Hexham. He appears to have been well connected, for he was a lifelong friend of King David I of Scotland and the king's son, Henry, whose dominions stretched far south across what was later to be the border. Ailred passed from boyhood to manhood and was appointed seneschal of Scotland. He relinquished a brilliant career at court to become a monk when, in 1134, he entered the great and beautiful Rievaulx in Yorkshire as a Cistercian. He left nine years later to become abbot of Ravesby in Lincolnshire. After four years he was back at Rievaulx as abbot.

Apart from his friendship with the royal family, Ailred had many Scottish links. He delighted in visiting Dundrennan and the other Scottish Cistercian houses, and he wrote the life of St Ninian which became the standard biography. He was a close friend of Godric, the hermit of Finchale.

His theological works showed not only great depth of learning, but also spirituality; foremost among these were *Speculum Caritatis* ('The Mirror of Charity') and *De Spirituali Amicitia* ('On Spiritual Friendship'). Among the finest gems of medieval devotion is his great pastoral prayer for his family of monks. An extract (translated) reads:

To Thee, my comfort and my God, I humbly own
That I am not as contrite and as fearful as I ought to be
For my past sins,
Nor do I feel enough concern about my present ones.
And Thou, Sweet Lord, hast set a man like this over thy
    family.
Me, who take all too little trouble with myself,
Thou biddest to be concerned on their behalf;
And me, who never pray enough about my own sins,
Thou wouldst have pray for them.
I, who have taught myself so little too,
Have also to teach them.
Wretch that I am, what have I done?
What have I undertaken? What was I thinking of?
Or rather, Sweet Lord, what wast Thou thinking of
Regarding this poor wretch?

Ailred died at Christmas 1166, prematurely worn out not only by his responsible monastic duties but by illness. From living for years in damp, cold buildings, he contracted very severe arthritis and internally he suffered from kidney and bladder disorders. His faithful biographer monk, Walter Daniel, tells a little about the beloved abbot's terrible pain, with constant rising during the night for relief.

Ailred was never formally canonised but from the beginning his Cistercian brethren accorded him the honours of a saint.

His festival is 3 March, or 3 February for the Cistercian order.

F. M. Powicke (ed), *The Life of Ailred of Rievaulx by Walter Daniel,* 1950

andRew The four constituent nations

of the British Isles have gone their own ways in selecting 'patrons' or protecting saints. England seems satisfied with the semi-mythical St George, rather a pantomime figure with his dragon, who never had the slightest connection with her history and whose traditions were almost all in eastern Europe. Ireland and Wales, in Patrick and David, have chosen saints who are local heroes and missionaries in these countries. Scotland alone has an apostle as patron, but one whom she has to share with Romania, Greece and the USSR. (We cannot emphasise often enough that Jesus' disciple, Andrew of Bethsaida, never had the faintest connection with Scotland or with the town in Fife which bears his name.)

Andrew, of course, was never chosen as patron by the Scottish people but was rather forced upon them as part of a propaganda drive to enhance the prestige of the new bishopric of St Andrews which the Church had decided must supersede the older Culdee or Celtic settlements at Dunkeld and Abernethy. In fact, it was not till several centuries after the coming of Christianity to our land that Andrew was singled out for special homage, or that any claim was made for his having any Scottish connection.

In the early Middle Ages the story was circulated that the saint's relics had been carried by a certain St Regulus to the shores of Fife, where his ship was forced to land by a fierce storm. The bones of the apostle were buried, in obedience to a vision, at Kilrymont where the great cathedral was built. In fact, Regulus (or Rule) was a Celtic missionary of many generations earlier whose name was introduced to give the fable an appearance of truth. He had his monastery on the river Shannon in Ireland at a place associated with an earlier missionary, Cainnech or Kenneth, who also figures prominently in the traditions of early Christianity in Fife. There is some reason to believe that traces of Kenneth's work were suppressed to make way for the new fabricated official history. Although Regulus may have had nothing to do with the transportation of the relics (which were vitally important to the new cathedral as they brought the pilgrims who brought the money) he must have had some important if now forgotten link with Kilrymont as the great isolated tower still standing beside the cathedral ruins, and the cave among the rocks, once visited by Dr Johnson, will testify. The various legends of a shipwreck should all be discounted, although they still appear to be taught to schoolchildren and still appear in the glossy guide books for tourists.

The most likely explanation of the story is that Scotland's link with the apostle Andrew came through St Acca, successor to Wilfred as abbot of Hexham in Northumberland. Wilfred founded two abbeys, Ripon and Hexham, naming the first after Peter, as first apostle, and the second after Peter's brother, Andrew. Bede, the historian, tells how Wilfred and Acca brought back from Rome a large number of saints' relics which they valued highly and venerated. Later when Acca met King Angus MacFergus it is probable that he gave or sold to the king some of the relics of St Andrew. Professor Skene suggested that Acca himself may have brought them to Kilrymont. Frank Knight linked the place-name Balhucca in Fife with the Northumbrian abbot.

Perhaps it is some lingering folk memory that this saint was a late arrival, or a suspicion that he had been imposed upon them that has made Scots much less mindful of their patron than the Irish or the Welsh. We seldom become enthusiastic or lyrical over Andrew except when we sing 'as of old St Andrew heard it', instead of 'apostles heard it', as the English and the others are singing. Andrew is not sung about in pubs as Patrick is, nor does the mention of him bring tears to the eyes of Scots as the mention of David does to Welshmen. Around the saint's day, 30 November, our clergy preach a few sermons, not usually of very high quality, in which Andrew's character is somehow likened to that of the typical Scot, and certainly he heads the list in possessing the largest number of church dedications, but otherwise it is mainly the Scots brethren overseas who remember St Andrew's day.

The best gift the saint has given Scotland is the Saltire, the white cross on blue. Strangely enough our covenanting forefathers, who had little use for saints, seem to have been very proud of the St Andrew Cross on their banners. Technically known in Christian art as the Crux Decussata, the linking of this type of cross with our saint comes late in the development of his legend. Its origin for Scotland is explained in the legend of Athelstaneford, the East Lothian village where the Anglian King Athelstane encamped before meeting King Angus and his Picts in battle. The historian Buchanan recounts the story:

> Hungus, worn out with bodily fatigue and mental anxiety, fell into a slumber in which there appeared to him Saint Andrew . . . who promised him a glorious victory. This vision flushed the Picts with hope and they prepared with alacrity for the conflict. . . . It is added that a decussated cross appeared in the sky which so terrified the English that they were scarcely able to withstand the first attack of the Picts. Hungus, who attributed the victory to St Andrew . . . appropriated to his service a tenth part of the royal demesnes.

The present *Church of Scotland Year Book* lists more than half a hundred parishes claiming the saint, but many of these are of recent date. The most dense cluster lies in the central and southern areas; Andrew is noticeably rarer in the Highlands and Islands. The Roman Catholics have two of their Scottish Cathedrals to Andrew and there are several other churches, including the Ukrainian Catholic Church in Edinburgh. Some mediaeval dedications have obviously been transferred to Andrew from earlier Celtic missionaries when the Church began to insist on an apostolic figure as patron. Eccles (Berwickshire) changed from St Cuthbert to St Andrew in 1250.

There are parishes of St Andrew, i.e. Kirkandrews, on the north bank of the Solway (now united with Borgue) and on the south, near Carlisle. There is a parish of St Andrew's in Orkney and Lhanbryde near Elgin includes an older parish of his name. There are parishes with commemorations to Andrew at Dirleton, Gullane, Eccles, Melville (Lasswade), Peebles, Carluke, Golspie, Bellie, Tyrie and Rayne. Monikie on the Tay opposite Kilrymont claims connection with the saint's shrine.

Of the life of the apostle the gospels say little. He seems to have ranked fourth among the Twelve, just outside the intimate trio of Peter, James and John. A native of Bethsaida, fisherman of Capernaum and brother to Simon Peter, he figures first as a follower of St John the Baptist (John 1: 29) then in Mark 1: 16 as leaving his nets to follow Jesus. He directed enquirers to Jesus in John 12: 21 and also the boy in the feeding of the five thousand (John 6: 8). Like all the apostles except John he fades quickly from the story of the Church, the tradition being that he was martyred at Patras in Achaia. An apochryphal 'Acts and Martyrdom of St Andrew' and other additions and inventions to his story are of no historical significance.

His festival is 30 November.

D. Attwater, *The Penguin Dictionary of Saints*, 1965

R. Kirk, *St Andrews*, 1954

J. M. Mackinlay, *Ancient Church Dedications in Scotland*, 1910

antony

This Egyptian hermit received enormous popular veneration during the Middle Ages. The earlier part of his life was spent in complete solitude in the desert, and he later withdrew to his 'inner mountain' (Colzim) near the Red Sea. His attempts at solitude were interrupted by sightseers, visitors and those seeking help, and a further disturbance came with a series of temptations. At the end of this period he founded a community of followers who had gathered round him. Later, Antony went to Alexandria and took a prominent part in controversy with the Arians. He died in 356, aged 105. His remains, lost for two centuries, were recovered and eventually restored at La Motte where the Order of Hospitallers of St Antony was founded in 1100.

Antony is represented on the Anglo-Saxon carvings on the great Ruthwell Cross in Dumfriesshire. On the slopes of Edinburgh's Arthur's Seat are ruins of a chapel dedicated to Antony, where, says tradition, a light used to be kept burning to guide ships into the harbour at Leith. The Knights of the Order had a preceptory in Leith, apparently an impressive building whose tower suffered destruction during the seige of that town. The gatehouse of the preceptory was known as St Antony's Port. He was specially honoured in sea-ports, and Leith had its own baron-bailie of St Antony.

His festival is 17 January.

J. Grant, *Old and New Edinburgh*, 1883
J. D. Douglas, *The New International Dictionary of the Christian Church*, 1974

aᴛheʀnaɪѕe The parish church of

Leuchars in Fife is dedicated to this saint about whom we know almost nothing. There are several versions of the name: in the *Felire of Oengus*, he appears as 'Ithernaisc nad labrae' ('Ithernaisc who spoke not') but we are without any clue as to why he did not speak—was it some defect, like St Fillan's, which rendered him mute?

In the mediaeval *Breviary* he receives an appropriate and touching collect:

O God, who didst will that the soul of blessed Ethernascus, Thy confessor, should penetrate to the stars of heaven, vouchsafe that, as we celebrate his venerable birthday, we may by his intercessions, be deemed worthy of Thy mercy, in respect of his merits meet to ascend to the joys of his blessed life, through Our Lord.

15

Little did the author of the collect think that the day would come when from the field next to Ithernaisc's church, men would penetrate very nearly 'to the stars of heaven' in machines of their own making.

Most renowned among the Leuchars' ministers was Alexander Henderson, moderator of the famous Glasgow Assembly of 1638 and probably most intellectual of the Covenanters. It is said that Henderson's face was 'yellow from the fever he contracted in the Leuchars' marshes', for the name means 'a marshy stream'. In 1763 Dr Johnson found time to call and have a chat with the minister at his manse. For long the wonderful chancel and apse, original Norman work, were boarded up, but during the present century a succession of caring ministers have beautified and restored the church.

Leuchars also has a connection with the crusades. At the end of the twelfth century the lands of Leuchars passed into the hands of the de Quinci family, and this family furnished a number of knights to the crusades. Evidence of this may be found in armorial bearings within the church.

There is a second dedication to Athernaise, jointly with St John the Evangelist, at the church of Lathrisk, also in Fife. The date of the dedication of Lathrisk was 1243 and Leuchars' dedication was a year later; both were due to King Alexander's chamberlain, David de Bernham.

Athernaise's festival is 22 December.

A. P. Forbes, *Kalendars of Scottish Saints*, 1872
Leuchars Church Handbook

ayle was one of the outstanding group of Irish missionaries who took the faith into the countries of the European continent. The leader of this group was St Columbanus of Bobbio. Ayle accompanied St Eustace to Bavaria where he became the pioneer missionary noted both for personal devotion and scholarship. He then penetrated to the further side of the Jura mountains to preach but returned to end his life preaching in Bavaria. He died about 650, near Meaux, aged 66.

It is not known why Ayle's cult became popular in Scotland. The abbey of Balmerino (or Balmerrinoch) in north Fife, and Anstruther in the south of the county both have evidence of the influence of the cult of St Ayle: there are chapels dedicated to him at Balmerino and at Anstruther-Easter, which also had St Ayle's croft and house. His name is found in several spellings: Yle, Yzle and even Teal, the usual name for him in Balmerino. Here the last letter of the word 'saint' has become affixed to the name. There is also Killmayaille in Kintyre with an ancient site.

Ayle's festival is on 30 August.

A. P. Forbes, *Kalendars of Scottish Saints*, 1872

G. A. F. Knight, *Archaeological Light on the Early Christianising of Scotland*, 1933

Baithene Traditionally one of the twelve who first crossed with Columba to Iona, Baithene (born in 536) is frequently mentioned by Adamnan. Said to be a younger cousin of Columba, he acted as head of the sub-community on Tiree and succeeded his cousin as abbot of the 'familia Chaluimchille'. However, he survived for only three years, dying on the same day as the saint.

Baithene was renowned for his prayerfulness. The tradition was that between each mouthful of food he was wont to exclaim, 'Deus in adjutorium meum intende' ('O God, come to my help'). At harvest as he gathered corn he held the sickle in one hand but kept the other arm raised to heaven in prayer. He fasted so often that when he rose from resting on the sand the prints of his ribs could clearly be seen. Warned by Columba on one occasion not to set sail to his farm on Tiree because a fierce beast was dangerously close by, Baithene launched his coracle, saying, 'That beast and I are both under the power of God'. Encountering the beast during the voyage, Baithene raised his hand and blessed the animal, which disappeared under the waves. When Columba died as he was transcribing Psalm 34, his last words, as the pen fell from his grasp, were, 'Let Baithene finish it'.

The *Felire of Oengus* pays tribute to both saints in one verse:

They went into the eternal kingdom,
Into eternal life of brightest splendour;
Baithene the noble, the angelical,
Columb-cille, the resplendent.

After his death in 600, Baithene was buried in St
Oran's chapel on Iona. His festival is naturally on
Columba's day.

A. O. and M. O. Anderson (eds), *Adomnan's Life of
Columba*, 1961

baldred

Two saintly men are held in special honour by the folk of East Lothian and treasured as peculiarly their own. The two were very different in their lives and in their beliefs: Baldred, an anchorite (hermit) who lived in the Dark Ages and Blackadder the Covenanter of the seventeenth century. Both were by family East Lothian men though their missionary journeys took them widely through the Borders and beyond. The grey cliffs of the Bass were home to both for at least a good portion of life: the hermit Baldred because he chose to have it that way, the Covenanter Blackadder because he was prisoned there till he died.

In this book we deal only with saints—at least with those to whom this title is generally given— and as the Reformed Churches forsook the privilege of naming anyone for this honour, John Blackadder remains uncanonised and so will receive no further mention here. This is quite likely as he would have wished it. Of Baldred we must tell a little more.

It was for long accepted that he had been a follower of St Kentigern and had worked with and under that great missionary around the beginning of the seventh century. However, recent research compels students of the period to forsake the dates in the *Aberdeen Breviary* and accept the dating of Simeon of Durham that Baldred died ('trod the way of the Holy Fathers' as Simeon so much more graciously puts it) 'in the 20th year of King Egbert of Northumbria', which marks it exactly as 756. Not much can be written about the life of an anchorite except that he fulfilled his chosen work in his chosen cell and passed on the missionary task to the next generation. Every generation, though, needs fresh conversions, for Dean Inge once wrote truly 'each generation represents a fresh invasion of the barbarians'.

It is clear that even Baldred did not spend all his years in his cave for he has left several place-names in East Lothian suggesting his presence. Baldred's Chapel at Tantallon is now little more than a ruin. At Aldham Bay you may see the rock called Baldred's boat when the tide is out. Like other mediaeval saints, if no boat was handy he just sailed over on a rock. 'Baldred's Cradle', further down the coast, is a terrifying fissure in the rocks through which the tides roar when the storms come. Prestonkirk and Tyning-ham parishes have many memorials of Baldred and the kirk at the former place may well be the site of his chapel. His huge stone image is said to have lain there till 1770 when a new kirk was built and a mason, perhaps inspired by shades of Blackadder, took a hammer and broke the image up.

His festival day is 6 March.

A. P. Forbes, *Kalendars of Scottish Saints*, 1872

G. A. F. Knight, *Archaeological Light on the Early Christianising of Scotland*, 1933

beᵹa

Although this female saint appears to have made her headquarters on the coast of

Cumbria she was remembered and venerated during the Middle Ages on the Scottish side of the border. The traditions and legends which gathered round her name told how, sometime in the seventh century, Bega crossed from the Strangford district of County Down, landed near the rocky headland later known as Saint Bee's Head and settled nearby, either as a solitary recluse or, more probably, as leader of a small female religious community. We should discount the usual hagiological trimmings that she sailed across the channel miraculously floating on a leaf, and that when she requested ground for her cell she was told to use what remained of the winter snowflakes on a summer day. We shall find that a similar crossing was attributed to Modwenna and other female voyagers. These items from the stock in hand of every mediaeval hagiographer do not die easily and keep reappearing in various forms to excite the credulous and amuse sceptics.

Whether Bega laboured alone or was joined by other devout women, she laboured at St Bee's long enough for her name to become associated with the place ever since. We next find her as one of the little circle of women, led and inspired by St Aidan. This circle included Ebba of St Abb's, Hilda of Whitby (in Northumbria it is said that Bega assisted and deputised for Hilda at Whitby), Ethelreda of Ely and others. It has been said that Bega owed her conversion to Aidan but we believe she may have been a Christian before she crossed from Ireland, for the Strangford Lough area traced its converts back to and beyond St Patrick's preaching. St Bee's in Cumbria remained conscious of its links with Nendrum, the Strangford monastery, whose founder Mochaoi, a youthful disciple of Patrick, had, like Bega, crossed the channel and laboured beside the Solway. Probably Bega brought her Irish Celtic strain of Christianity to the Saxon church and its small but very vigorous group of abbesses.

There are also place-names which suggest that Bega may have moved round parts of Scotland. Some of these we may pass over as probably the result of later veneration for her memory, but others seem to have their origin in Celtic times.

Eastward from Broughton, down the valleys of the Tweed and the Lyne we find several Bega place-names: at Drumelzier and Stobo (places reminiscent of Merlin and his wizardry), on to Kilbucho with a St Bee's Well, then further afield Eddleston, Gillebechistoun ('the town of Bega's servant'), we trace such names down the valleys. More doubtfully, we could continue as far as Clackmannan and Argyll.

Probably the successor to Bega's first simple cell at St Bee's continued to give shelter to religious folk, off and on, till about 1225 when the new centralised and efficient mediaeval church established a Benedictine community at the spot. This was placed under the care of the powerful St Mary's abbey in York. In the charters of the Norman Thomas de Courcy we find that two-thirds of the lands of the island of 'Neddrum' are granted to St Mary's of York and St Bega of Coupland, and this is repeated in several later documents—thus preserving right to the end of the Middle Ages the ancient link between the old Patrician monastery in County Down and the seventh-century community at St Bee's.

St Bega's festival day is 31 October.

C. Cox, *County Churches: Cumberland and Westmorland,* 1913

H.C. Lawlor, *The Monastery of St Mochaoi,* 1925

J. Parker, *Cumbria*, 1977
E. S. Towill, 'St Mochaoi and Nendrum' in *Ulster Journal of Archaeology*, 1964

ƀlane and catan As these

two sixth-century missionaries were so closely related both by blood and by their spheres of labour, it is convenient to study them together. Catan, tradition states, was a member of the most extensive of all Celtic 'muinntirs' or monasteries, at Bangor in County Down. He resolved to 'peregrinare pro Christo', to go 'a-wandering for Christ', which was not unusual for monks at that date. Many of these Irish monks made extensive journeys and tried out many places before eventually finding a suitable site for a new foundation. Catan indeed may have done just this, for many place-names in Argyll and west Scotland could refer to him. In the end he found the site he wanted not too far from Bangor, at Kilchattan Bay at the south end of the island of Bute. Here he set up his community within a 'rath' or enclosure which can still be traced.

Tradition states that Catan was accompanied by his sister, Ertha or Bertha, a sensible custom sometimes met with among the Celtic missionaries, for such a woman would be invaluable in arranging the good ordering of the new community. The story then alleges that Ertha became pregnant by an unknown man—one version claims that it was Aedan, King of the Scots—and as punishment her brother Catan, with Celtic severity, set her and her new-born son adrift in an oarless boat which was eventually driven ashore on the Ulster coast. There the saints Kenneth and Comgall received them and determined to educate the boy, Blane, at Comgall's great

23

monastery of Bangor. This part of the traditional story must be treated with reservation as the idea of a hero drifting in an oarless boat is a common Celtic folk-myth associated with various figures, e.g. Maughold of Man, and Enoch and Kentigern. After his training under Comgall and perhaps under Kenneth at Aghaboe, Blane returned to Bute where he was reunited with his uncle Catan whose work he developed and extended.

While there may be doubt about the historical truth of the details and the exact dates when these saints worked, there can be no doubt about the importance of the settlement at Cean-garadh (Kingarth) on Kilchattan Bay. There were also dozens of satellite foundations throughout Argyll which took the name of one or other of the founders. In time Blane moved eastward to Strathearn and the district known as Fortriu where it is now believed Gaidheals from the west were replacing the Pictish settlements; perhaps part of Blane's purpose was to minister to these people as he himself was probably of Irish Cruithnean or Pictish stock.

In this area Blane is specially remembered for the foundation by the banks of the Allan Water which was to become the great Dunblane cathedral. There is some evidence to suggest that the original settlement was on higher ground slightly to the north of the present Scottish Churches' House, where some traces of the mediaeval buildings have been uncovered. Around the Fintry Hills was another district evangelised by Blane, and the place-names, Blanefield, Strathblane etc, are significant. A gloss in the *Felire of Oengus* after Blane has 'Blaan the mild, of Mingarth and Dunblane was his chief monastery and of Kingarth is he'. One tradition gives Dunblane as Blane's resting place but another says that a stone sarcophagus at St Blaan's church, Kingarth holds his bones. There are other supposed Blane sites widely scattered through the mainland.

Catan is remembered more in the islands. Colonsay has the remains of a chapel and a stone called Cruidhe Chattan (Catan's Heel); Cill-Cathain is at Kildalton in Islay, with chapel ruins; and Kilchattan was formerly the title of a parish in Jura. There is also Ardchattan Priory by Loch Etive and other mainland sites.

Festival for Blane is 11 or 10 August.

J. H. Cockburn, *The Celtic Church in Dunblane*, 1954

G. A. F. Knight, *Archaeological Light on the Early Christianising of Scotland*, 1933

ᛒᴏɪꜱɪʟ This quiet, unassuming monk has given his name to the small but prosperous community of St Boswells. We have known men in our day not unlike Boisil, who pass unnoticed in a crowd and remain ignored when they try to speak at meetings but who quietly take charge when things go wrong.

Boisil succeeded Eata as abbot of Old Maelros, the original monastery which was later moved to a more convenient site. While he was prior under Eata he watched the young Cuthbert approach and greeted him with the prophetic words 'Behold the servant of the Lord'. Bede calls him 'a man of remarkable piety, a monk and priest of surpassing merit and gifted with a prophetic faculty.' He seems to have laboured mainly around Melrose. As well as St Boswells the kirk at Lessuden in Roxburgh is also his. He foretold the coming of the dreaded yellow plague of which he himself became a victim in 661 or 664.

25

Before he died, he read the Gospel of John with Cuthbert.

His festival day is 23 February.

G. A. F. Knight, *Archaeological Light on the Early Christianising of Scotland*, 1933

bonach was chaplain at the chapel

'situate et fundate intra villam de Lucheria', which seems to have been a chapel distinct from the Leuchars parish church and situated where later the school was built. Among miscellanea in St Andrews university library there is reference in the fifteenth century to a relic of 'Sancti Bonoci episcopi' which cannot imply that Bonach had been bishop in the sense which was accepted by the fifteenth century, the full monarchical episcopate, but that he held episcopal orders in the much simpler Celtic set-up. His date was probably the early years of the eighth century and (on very slight supporting evidence) Frank Knight identifies him with the Benedictus who was among the party which St Curitan brought up from Northumbria with the object of introducing the Roman customs into the Pictish Kingdom.

Bonach certainly left an impression on the district—there is a St Bunnow's or Bonach's Hill and there was an annual fair named after him. Across the firth at Invergowrie is a Balbunnoch. The nature of Bonach's chapel and chaplaincy are not known but may have been connected with the de Quincis or other local family. It is not likely that it was the predecessor of the parish church which in 1244 was dedicated to St Athernaise, for the latter is on a very obvious Celtic site while Bonach's chapel was elsewhere.

A. P. Forbes, *Kalendars of Scottish Saints*, 1872
G. A. F. Knight, *Archaeological Light on the Early Christianising of Scotland*, 1933

bRendan There are two saints called

Brendan in the sixth–seventh centuries. We are only concerned here with the most famous, St Brendan of Clonfert. He achieved wide popularity in the Middle Ages through various collections of stories of his wonderful 'voyages' and became as illustrious in the world of exploration and travelling as did King Arthur in the world of chivalry.

Brendan was born, say the mediaeval lives, near Tralee in the Shannon estuary. He was trained under Bishop Erc, later under St Ita at Killeedy and then at the great monastic seminary of Clonard. Some biographers take him as far as the Welsh monastery of Llancarfan to complete his studies. He set out early in life on his 'peregrination', the journeying for Christ which was the usual sixth-century pattern of ministry for a Celtic missionary. Dangerous sailings through treacherous straits between the islets and across the competing tides in more open waters seemed to worry Brendan even less than they did the other monastic brethren. He founded churches along the coasts of his own island and also further inland. When he crossed to Scotland he sailed among the western isles founding churches, perhaps even rounding the Pentland Firth and sailing down the east coast. Such was his later fame that it is now almost impossible to separate the later place-names from those genuine and contemporary with the saint. One scholar, Dr Pochin Mould, accepted those on the west of Scotland but remained sceptical about those on the east coast.

Brendan's great reputation, however, did not depend on such short journeys, difficult and dangerous as they might be in a curragh. His classic voyages consisted traditionally of two journeys of two and five years duration respectively, one in a large skin-covered curragh, the other in a larger wooden boat with more companions. They were the science fiction of their day and still provide exciting reading. Commentators have varied greatly in their interpretation of the reality behind the stories. One of the most penetrating analyses of the voyages was made at the beginning of this century by John, third Marquess of Bute, who after detailed study came to the conclusion that any such voyages would be completely impossible even now and the whole thing, he thought, was intended to be fiction, into which two or three factual incidents had been incorporated. However, in 1976–7 the marquess was proved quite wrong when a party of men, led by Tim Severin, set out from Galway and sailed north up the west coast of Scotland, then headed out across the Atlantic, by Iceland and Greenland, in the path of St Brendan. They sailed in as exact a replica of Brendan's larger boat as they could construct. The voyage stretched over two seasons, with the party wintering en route, but in the end they made it and beached their small craft off the American coast. Tim Severin's account of the journey is as thrilling a story as you will find. He also includes a condensed translation of the mediaeval *Navagatio*, and many of the incidents in the old monkish chronicle fit in with those which today's travellers met. We may still interpret the *Navigatio* in differing ways: it could be an amalgam of myth and legend from many sources; it could be the Christianised version of an Irish folk-tale; but it could well be, as Severin proved, a largely factual experience.

Brendan is well remembered in Scotland as well as Ireland. The great stretch of water separating Arran from Kintyre is called Kilbrannan Sound, and looking down on this from Kilpatrick in Arran there stands a great cashel which may have surrounded the saint's community or 'muinntir'. Along the sound are two creeks or harbours called Brann-a-Phuirt and Brian Puirt. The islands are dotted with his chapels—on Tiree, Islay, Barra, St Kilda. On Elachnave there is a monastery near Dun-Bhrenain. On Mull Kilbrandan is in Kilninian parish. Seil island has a similarly named site with ruins of an ancient church. Although the island of Bute's name does not derive from the saint, as is sometimes suggested, he is patron of the island. A Rothesay church bears his name and islanders are still Brandanes.

On Aileach an Naoimh in the Garvelloch isles Brendan was present at the Mass of the Saints. Down in Kirkcowan (Wigtownshire) we have a Drummelbrennan, while if we go over to the north-east, Boyndie (Banffshire) recognised Brendan as patron, and nearby was a St Brandon's Haven. The old church at Birnie near Elgin was called Brennach. The list of commemorations of various kinds could be still further extended but we just note finally that in Fife, Kirkcaldy has a fair named after him and Markinch has a Balbirnie Burn.

Brendan's festival day is 16 May.

S. Baring-Gould and J. Fisher, *The Lives of the British Saints*, 1913
C. Plummer (ed.), *Vitae Sanctorum Hiberniae*, 1969
T. Severin, *The Brendan Voyage*, 1975

ᏰᏒᎥᎠᎬ ᎾᏒ ᏰᏒᎥᎠᎶᎬᏖ

There are several Brides, Brigits, Bridgets or Bridhdes. There is the historical saint, the legendary goddess and the popular cultic figure who is an amalgam of the goddess and perhaps early Christian saints. We shall deal here with all three.

The legendary, pre-Christian Celtic Brigit was the goddess daughter of the great Dagda, lord of the Earth, powerful as the fire-goddess among the Tuatha-De-Danaan. To conciliate the Femors, the sea giants, they married her to Bress, son of the Femor leader and she became mother to Ruadan, half giant, half god. She gave her name to the important British tribe the Brigantes as their tutelary goddess and is the Celtic counterpart of the Roman Minerva.

The historic St Bridget of Kildare (c. 452–524) was born to Brocessa, the Christian slave of a pagan bard, Dubhach. Conflicting traditions put her birth-place at Dundalk or near Kildare where most of her life was to be spent. Sold as a slave to a Druid master, her gentleness and goodness won him over to Christianity and she and her mother were set free. 'The picture we get', writes Dr Pochin Mould, 'is of yet another bastard child growing up in the Kildare plains, helping her mother with the cattle, herding and milking them and making butter.' She resisted efforts to get her to marry and, determined to take the vow of perpetual virginity, made her way to Ardagh. By some mistake, continues the tradition, Bishop Mel read the wrong service over her and she received consecration as a bishop, an office she was allowed to retain because of her sanctity. The story savours of the apocryphal and may have been an attempt to explain Bridget's supposed leadership of a mixed community of monks and nuns. It was not, however, till twenty years later that she founded her monastic community. Meantime she returned to her girlhood district and moved about the Curragh, deservedly acquiring a reputation for gracious, kindly and saintly deeds which later were woven into Irish folk-lore. About 490 she was given land at Cill-Dara, the church of the oak, and began to gather the people and the material for the simple monastery of little huts and oratories which after her day was to become one of the great Irish monastic institutions.

Scholars have suggested that the saint's very simple original monastery did not become open to both sexes until later but the tradition has become established that she appointed Conlaedh as coadjutor-bishop to oversee the male inmates. Her biographer, Cogitosus, who wrote for her the first 'life' of any Irish saint, left us a good description of the monastery and the life within and in his day it was clearly coeducational. However, that was a century and a half later.

The popular, devotional figure, so reverenced throughout Ireland and in the Catholic isles of Scotland and found in every corner of the land in a multitude of place-names, draws largely on what is known of Bridget of Kildare's life story but it also incorporates features of the Celtic goddess—there is evidence that at the Kildare monastery for some centuries a perpetual fire was kept burning; she was supposed to have been born at sunrise; a house where she dwelt blazed with a great light; a pillar of fire arose from her brow when she took the veil—all obvious links with the fire-goddess.

It is unlikely that the abbess of Kildare was ever in Scotland, yet there are so many dedications to her that some have supposed that there were others of the same name, or that traditions of other godly women became attached to the original Bridget. Her feast falls on 1 February while the pagan Candlemas, later adopted by Christians, falls just one day later. Bridget is accepted in Ireland as the protector of newly-sown crops, almost a fertility goddess. On the eve of her day people make little rush crosses, including the beautiful 'triskele', and these are blessed at her mass in church.

As we would expect, it is in Wigtownshire and round the Solway that the frequency of her commemorations is greatest, but it is in the Gaelic Highlands and islands that the mention of Bride raises a tear, or a song, or an oft-repeated story. Particularly in those islands where tradition has not been erased by centuries of Protestantism, she is 'Muime Chriosd', foster-mother to the infant Jesus, or she is Mary of the Gael, or Bride the calm one of the smooth, white palms and the clustering gold-brown hair. The least fulsome and most loving tribute is from the book of Lismore:

> She was abstinent, she was innocent, she was prayerful, she was patient, she was glad in God's commandments, she was firm, she was humble, she was forgiving, she was loving, she was a consecrated casket for keeping Christ's Body and His Blood, she was a Temple of God. Her heart and her mind were a Throne of Rest for the Holy Ghost.

Natives of Colonsay formerly kept a Candlemas custom known as Bride's Bed. A sheaf of corn dressed in women's clothes was put in a large basket along with a wooden club and the household, before retiring, chanted 'Bride is come; Bride is welcome'. Next morning they looked among the ashes in the grate for an imprint of the club; if there was none they feared a poor crop.

The *Church of Scotland Year Book* lists eleven parish churches bearing her name (there are also as many dedications to Bride on the English shore of the Solway as on the Scottish; in Wales her dedications are often as Ffraid Santes). There are Kilbrides and Kirkbrides too numerous to mention. Brydekirk is near Annan, and Briddeburgh is not far away; Panbride is in Angus and in Fife there is Pitlumbertie. Near the Forth Bridge is the ancient St Bride's chapel at Dalgety. The parish church of Blair Atholl was Bridget's. A most likely place to have some real connection with the saint is Abernethy by the Tay: by the sixth century or earlier the Celtic monastery there was linked with her name and the seal of the later priory had her figure with a cow, which was one of her symbols, beside her. In County Down, a huge boulder outside Downpatrick Cathedral is, quite falsely, claimed as the burial place of Patrick, Columba and Bride.

D. Pochin Mould, *The Irish Saints*, 1964

ᏮRIOC is one of the most interesting but most difficult Celtic saints to study. We find his name appearing right across the Celtic world, but Scottish scholars know him as the patron saint of Rothesay and also find traces of his cult at Montrose (Inchbrayock Island) and Kirkcudbright (Dunrod). Most probably he is the same person as St Bryan of Maisterton near Dalkeith. Tradition also regards him as identical with the Brittany St Brieux and centres his work there. In Wales he plays a prominent part as Briog, and E. G. Bowen suggests he arrived in Wales from Cornwall, where he has several ancient dedications. Only from the records of the Goidhealic missionaries of Ireland is he noticeably absent, which is what we might expect as his name is Brythonic or Cumbric.

33

Tradition places him early among the saints, and makes him a disciple of the great Germanus, who arrived with him on his first British visit in 429. It would be an interesting work, but unfortunately one almost entirely of the imagination, to compose a composite biography from the various strands in his life-story. Professor Bowen is wisely cautious and avoids hagiology by classing him simply as one of the 'perigrini', the travelling missionaries.

His festival is 29–30 April.

E. G. Bowen, *Britain and the Western Seaways*, 1972

E. G. Bowen, *Settlements of the Celtic Saints in Wales*, 1955

A. P. Forbes, *Kalendars of Scottish Saints*, 1872

G. A. F. Knight, *Archaeological Light on the Early Christianising of Scotland*, 1933

ᏝRᎩᏟᎬ We might ask what Kirkcaldy has done to deserve Bryce for its patron saint. In most communities we find one member who manages to make himself objectionable to the rest; of Bryce, comments range from 'a real menace' to 'certainly an objectionable fellow, well intentioned but difficult'.

Surveying the few biographical details we have suggests of Bryce that few saints have possessed fewer saintly qualities. Laura Richards once wrote a book entitled *The Grumpy Saint* and if history be correct Bryce would easily qualify for this title. He was a follower of Martin of Tours, and assisted him as what we would call a 'suffragan'. Eventually he succeeded him in the see. The only remark of Martin about his assistant is revealing: 'If Christ endured Judas must not I endure Bryce.' He certainly was an outspoken critic of his boss which perhaps accounted for Martin's remark.

Educated at Marmoutier, Bryce had an even longer episcopate than Martin. Once he was accused of adultery but was acquitted at Rome. Following this ordeal he behaved more quietly and became very popular with the people for his missionary zeal. After his death he was venerated as a saint. In Kirkcaldy a church was named after him and Kirkmabreck in Galloway may come from his name.

His festival is 13 November.

D. H. Farmer, *Oxford Dictionary of Saints*, 1978

G. A. F. Knight, *Archaeological Light on the Early Christianising of Scotland*, 1933

Cecilia Patroness of music, especially of the organ, this third-century maiden martyr was betrothed to a young Roman named Valerian. Both he and his brother appear to be historical characters but Cecilia herself cannot provide any confirmation of her life or her martyrdom.

During her wedding ceremony she was said to have 'sung to the Lord in her heart'. Rather inconsiderately and inconsistently, we feel, Cecilia refused to honour her betrothal and to consummate the marriage. At this point her pagan spouse became a Christian and both he and his brother were executed by the emperor while the maiden was ordered to be steamed to death in her bathroom. When the heat seemed not to affect her, the axe was used, but so clumsily that she lingered half alive for three days.

Some two centuries later her cult began to spread rapidly but not till several centuries later did her connection with music and song become accepted. Chaucer's *Second Nun's Tale* deals with Cecilia's life; Dryden's 'Song for St Cecilia's Day' and a similar ode by Pope are among many tributes to this popular saint.

Edinburgh, as a cultural capital, held her in special honour and in 1762 built St Cecilia's Hall for concerts and musical performances. Works by Corelli, Handel and other musicians were regularly performed in the acoustically excellent oval-shaped hall. By the beginning of this century the hall was in danger of demolition, but the University acquired the building and they have restored it worthily to make it once again a place of good music.

Cecilia's festival day is 22 November.

J. Grant, *Old and New Edinburgh*, 1883
C. Williams, *Saints: Their Cults and Origins*, 1980

chRistopheR The story of Christopher belongs more to the literature of folklore and legend than to church history. According to legend Retrobus (later Christopher) was of giant stature but limited intelligence. As a youth he determined to serve the most powerful master he could find. After attaching himself for a time to an eastern potentate he noticed that his master trembled at the mention of the devil, so he left his service and from then onward sought only to serve Satan in any evil work. Eventually, however, he observed the devil trembling at the sight of the Christian Cross and so Retrobus determined to serve Christ. No one was able to show him where to find his new master, so meantime he contented himself with trying to do what good he could. Because of his great size and strength, this was the task of wading across a great river where there was neither bridge or ford, carrying travellers on his broad back and shoulders. One night in the darkness he heard a child crying to be carried across. He easily picked up the little one and carried him. Soon, however, he was surprised at the great weight which almost bore him down. Only with difficulty did he reach the opposite bank, where the infant revealed himself to be Jesus. From that time

Retrobus took the name Christopher, Christ Bearer.

He is reputed to have suffered martyrdom by being set up as a target for archery at Lycia in Asia Minor in the third century. His symbol is a flowering staff, as the legend claimed that the staff he used to steady himself against the river-current took root and blossomed like Aaron's rod.

Christopher became the patron of travellers, and even to look on a picture or statue of the saint was considered protection from danger for the day. This was of real concern to travellers in times when a journey of only a short distance presented real danger, and now that travelling is again increasingly hazardous the popularity of St Christopher medallions is on the increase. Few mediaeval churches were without a wall-painting or statue of the saint, painted or affixed opposite the entrance so that it might be seen even without entering the church. Most of these were erased at the Reformation but one of the best surviving ones may be seen in South Wales in the ancient church of St Illtyd at Llantwit Major. A giant Christopher dwarfing the other wall figures carries the Christ Child who holds the orb of the world, hence the weight which troubled Retrobus—and the artist has contrived that the saint is looking at the child while bearing him on his back; no easy placing of a model, one would imagine. An eel has wrapped itself round a leg of the saint and he holds the blossoming rod. The mural dates from about 1400.

There was always some doubt about the status of Christopher as his story was so largely legendary. He was classed among the fourteen Auxiliary Saints, known as the 'holy helpers', who were commonly invoked in devotion. In

1969 the saint was dropped from the Roman kalendar in the demoting of saints of doubtful historicity.

Today two Church of Scotland congregations bear the saint's name. Formerly he was connected with the parish of Cupar, and as late as 1614 there is reference to 'St Christopher's kirkzeard' at that place. St Magnus, Orkney, had a chapel to Christopher, as had St Nicholas, Aberdeen. In the isles he is commemorated at Uig on Lewis and at Barra. There were altars to him in Peebles, Irvine and St Giles.

Such was the saint's reputation for size that the Jesuits of Munich in the seventeenth century were said to display the bones of an elephant as his relics.

F. L. Cross and E. A. Livingstone (eds), *Oxford Dictionary of the Christian Church*, 1974
J. M. Mackinlay, *Ancient Church Dedications in Scotland*, Vol 2, 1914

COLM Down the east coast of Scotland we find a number of dedications to a Colm, Colme or Comb, and too often it has been supposed that the reference is to Columba or Columcille of Iona. A glance at the map of Scotland will show down the west coast an amazing cluster of sites to Columba and these are all in some variation of Kilcolmkil, the Gaelic form as we would expect. As Columba did not speak the language of east Scotland and made few journeys east of Drumalbyn we are justified in thinking that there was some other saint with a name like 'Colm' to whom these dedications should apply. Colman was a common name among the Irish saints; in the martyrologies we find some hundred different

Colmans. It has been suggested that the east coast Colm was one of 'Drostan's three' and that it is he who is referred to in Kirkcolm (Wigtownshire), Inchcolm island and similar places in Angus, Aberdeenshire, and so on. A. B. Scott believes there may be two distinct saints with this or similar names.

The figure is so hypothetical we cannot assign a festival date to it.

G. A. F. Knight, *Archaeological Light on the Early Christianising of Scotland*, 1933
A. B. Scott, *The Pictish Nation*, 1918

colman Almost a hundred saints of

this name are recorded in the Irish martyrologies. Colman of Lindisfarne succeeded Finan as abbot in 661 and in the controversy about Celtic versus Roman usages he supported the Celtic side against Wilfred and the Romanists. When eventually the ruling was in favour of the more universal Roman rites, Colman left Lindisfarne, taking all the Irish monks who had sided with him and also about thirty Anglians who held the same views. Carrying some of the relics of Iona abbey, they migrated to the small island of Inishbofin. Disagreement between the two groups caused the Anglians to leave to form their own community on the mainland opposite the island where the Irish monks established their own group. Not only was the Christian witness left shattered and divided, the last years of a wise and able abbot were clouded and his work cut short.

He died in 676 on 8 August, and his festival is 18 February.

H. Mayr-Harting, *The Coming of Christianity*, 1972

colmanella Called by Adamnan

Columbanus, filius Beognai, it is as well that in the biography of Columba we have in two places a positive identification as to which of the many Colmans in the Irish records the stories relate. His father Beognus was of the Ui-Neill clan, his mother is said to have been Columba's sister. The boy Colman was born in Glenelly where his father had taken refuge during a period of local warfare. The title Colman-ella arose because he made his chapel beside the small river Ela at the place known later as Lynally. In addition to his founding of communities at Lynally, Connor and Muckamore, he worked under Columba in Iona and so appears twice in Adamnan's pages. Once, when caught in a fierce storm off Rathlin island, he appealed to Columba and was told to pray more fervently for safety. The second occasion created something of a dilemma for Columba, who had chosen on the same day to send Columbanus, as Columba called him, to Ireland while posting Baithene in the opposite direction to Tiree. In the morning the wind was favourable for Tiree, and Columba noted in the afternoon when Baithene was safely landed that the wind changed and Colmanella could safely set off for Ireland. Incidentally, telling this story Adamnan makes it clear that at the time both saints were presbyters, not bishops.

Colmanella has a parish named for him, at Southend in Kintyre was a Kilcalmanell chapel and a third related place-name is at West Loch Tarbert. He is said to have been author of an *Alphabet of Devotion.*

The saint died on 26 September 611.

A. O. and M. O. Anderson (eds), *Adomnan's Life of Columba,* 1961

coLumba

This is the holy presbyter, Columba, the Arch-priest,
(uasal-sagart) of the island of the Gael, Colum-Cille, son
of Fedlimid, son of Fergus Ceunfada, son of Conall
Gulban, son of Neill of the Nine Hostages. Noble then was
his kindred as regards the world. By right of birth he was
fit to be chosen for the kingship of Ireland, and it would
have been offered to him had he not put it from himself for
the sake of God.

This is how the *Irish Life* manuscript in the
National Library of Scotland introduces the most
illustrious of Celtic missionary saints. But to keep
something like a true perspective, before we join
O'Donnell of the *Irish Life* and the host of
modern writers in saying lots of nice things about
this Irish prince and cleric, we should glance at
three rather different estimates of Columba.

I still keep a letter written to me by the late
John Mackechnie of the Aberdeen University
Celtic Department. Very much the most radical
of Celtic history scholars, Mackechnie's letter
reads: 'to say the least it is very odd that a
Christian teacher, said to be a male, should be
called after the bird dedicated to the pagan
goddess of love, and that he should set up a
centre at a Celtic "otherworld" e.g. the Mons
Angelorum, in an island called after the yew tree
and probably a centre of Yew Tree worship . . .
the horse weeping on Columba's bosom is
merely a version of a well-known episode in the
Tain.' For Mackechnie, Columba, Patrick, Kentigern and most of the others were merely
folk-myths and he remained disappointed that no
students of the Celtic saints took his efforts at
demythologising seriously.

Mackechnie, however extreme, is a relief from
the general chorus of adulation of Columba, but
he went beyond what legitimate criticism would

allow. Scrape away the legends which have grown up round the saint and Columba, a very real person, remains. Now, perhaps, the balance has been redressed. In his book *Columba*, Ian Finlay presents Columba as a very real person but one still surrounded by and influenced by a powerful body of pagan myth and legend. He argues that all the popular pictures must be redrawn: 'the familiar St Columba comes very near to being a myth, the real man has been obscured—some would say beyond recall.'

Finlay illustrates how near the world of paganism came to the Christian Columba, who, like Patrick, thought of himself as Christ's druid. There is an ominous legend or folk tale about the saint's arrival on the island. One Odhran, perhaps himself a monk, decides that the cemetery (which was later named after him) must have a sacrifice to consecrate it, and he volunteers to let himself be smothered with the soil of Iona and be buried there. We are forced to ask what truth, if any, lies behind this tale. Reading the lives of Columba one feels that it has been somehow transposed from a very much earlier age and involves a different Odhran from the one that followed Columba. There is no evidence or even any suggestion that the saint or anyone near him accepted human sacrifice, but we must admit that the folk tale is a strange one and demands some explanation. Finlay points to pagan influence in Celtic sculpture and art and suggests, perhaps a little humorously, that had Columba at any point made a false move we might today be examining his shrunken skull in a museum.

A third critic of Columba, Dr A. B. Scott, attacked on an entirely different front, and his prejudices do not deserve to be considered alongside the arguments of Finlay. Scott, arguing with some scholarship for the prior work of Ninian and Candida Casa, identified Columba, the Gael, with all Irishmen, some of whom had committed what to Scott was the gravest treachery—remaining aloof from Britain in the first Great War.

We must turn now to a short examination of problems about Columba which most biographies leave unsolved. Born at Garten in Donegal, Columba (or Columcille as the Irish invariably address him) early 'offered himself to the Lord of the Elements and begged three boons of Him: chastity and wisdom and pilgrimage'. He was educated at three of the great Irish seats of learning Magh Bile, Clonard and Glasnevin, and then went on to found a series of monasteries which were to form the powerful 'Parouchia Chaluimchille' (or 'family of Columba') which brought new impetus and vigour to Irish Christianity and supplemented and in some places supplanted the old Patrician settlements of Nendrum, Downpatrick and Killala. Adamnan's *Life of Columba,* the authority most often consulted for popular articles about the saint, spares little space for his activities in Ireland but the *Irish Life* tells of the first of his foundations in Derry:

> For this do I love Derry,
>   For its smoothness, for its purity,
> Because it is quite full of white angels
>   From one end to the other.

Other foundations followed—at Raphoe, Durrow, Swords and elsewhere—before he set sail for Scotland.

The reason for his going remains obscure. There is a story that he illicitly copied the manuscript of the new Jerome version of the Psalms and this so angered Finian that a great clan battle took place at Cooldrebhne, with Columba playing knight of the Ui Neill clan rather than acting like a leader of Christian clerics. In penitence, so the story goes, Columba chose self-exile. This story is difficult to accept. Long before, Columba had sworn 'to go a wandering for Christ', which was the usual pattern of life for Irish monastics of the time. There was indeed a great battle in the shadow of Ben Bulben, but the probable reason why Columba crossed to Argyll was a request or command from his king to act as adviser, in a political and religious capacity, to the Gaelic settlement in Scottish Dalriada. As a prince and also a cleric, Columba was well fitted to the task.

The *Irish Life* tells us that he 'left in Derry a cleric of his household, Da Cuilen, as his co-arb', and probably he did the same for his other foundations, leaving deputy abbots but retaining overall authority. It is incorrect, therefore, to picture Columba in Iona cutting himself off for ever from Ireland. Think of him rather as the religious leader of a powerful group of monasteries scattered throughout Ireland and loosely held together from Iona. Derry was more accessible from Iona than from Skellig Michael in Kerry, and Iona was not thought of as being in a foreign country. Nor was it by any means as cut off from either the Scottish or the Irish mainlands at the end of the sixth century as it was at the beginning of the twentieth century.

A verse from the *Irish Life* reads:

> Wondrous the warriors who abode on I,
> Thrice fifty in monastic rule,
> With their hearts on the main sea—
> Three score men a-rowing.

This does not suggest that Iona for the monks was

a place of seclusion but rather an active and virile community. It must not be forgotten, however, that it was also a place of study and retreat for meditation, scholarship and the necessary task of copying manuscripts. So thorough was Viking destruction in the ninth and tenth centuries that it is impossible now to know if the Columban scholars produced illuminated work of the standard of Kells, Durrow or Lindisfarne or annals and writings as important as those turned out at the Irish centres.

How far the saint himself or his immediate disciples evangelised Scotland, particularly the Pictish districts, is still a matter of debate among scholars. It seems that only rarely did he cross Drumalbyn, and the genuine foundation names, like Kilchaluimchille, are all in the western isles or the Dalriadic western mainland. Commemorations in the east, as in such forms as Colm or Comb, may well refer to some other founder.

Columba's visit to Inverness to meet King Brude is well documented, though the ancient authorities differ as to when in the saint's ministry it took place. In dealing with the visit, which was of considerable political importance, Adamnan probably over-emphasised the part played by Columba, for elsewhere he does not appear as leader and chief spokesman but simply as one of the deputation. It is also improbable that the Pictish chieftain was so impressed that he became a Christian. One cannot doubt, however, that apart from any religious effect, the meeting had political implications for relations between the indigenous Picts and the recent immigrant Gaedhails.

Adamnan's *Life of Columba* is well worth reading, giving insight into life in a Celtic monastery, if not as it was in the founder's day at least as it was under Adamnan, the ninth abbot. It includes many anecdotes of the saint in his wanderings, although the narrative is well inter- laced with the prophecies, miracles and visions into which the author divided his book.

Surviving memorials of Columba are not numerous; there is the 'Cathach' or 'Battler', a portion of the psalms in a book-shrine which dates from the saint's day and traditionally was said to be the copy he made secretly in Finian's library which led to the battle of Cooldrebhne. Scholars seem more ready now than they were formerly to accept it as genuine. There are also two poems attributed to him—the short 'Noli Pater' and the 'Altus Prosator' which is an alphabetic effort in Latin, each stanza beginning with a different letter.

Columba crossed to Ireland to take part in the convention of Drumceatt in 575 at which ques- tions of the independence of Scottish Dalriada from Ireland and the future of the order of Bards were under discussion. He was still much in- volved in secular affairs, for four years later he supported the Ui Neill clan at the battle of Coleraine which arose from a dispute about one of Comgall's churches. In 585 he was back in Ireland inspecting his 'parouchia' and two years later was concerned with another battle, Cuil- fedha, between branches of his clan. While it is unlikely that he was present at either of these battles they show how false is the usual picture of Columba, divorced from the problems of the world, passing all his time in meditation on Iona. He was at times a very militant and active saint.

He died on 9 June 597 on his own island, with (says tradition) a summer storm blowing up and beating the waves in the sound so high that mourners could not cross the narrow strait. Adamnan's *Life* gives an almost hour to hour account of Columba's last days, but there is a more condensed version in the *Irish Life:*

> Now when Columcille came to his ending, and when the bell for Matins was struck on the night of Pentecost Sunday, he went before the rest to the church and made genuflexion and fervent prayer at the altar. Then an angelic radiance filled the church and the venerable old man sent forth his spirit into heaven, into the delight and into the joyance of heaven's household. His relics and holy remains are on earth with honour and reverence, with wonders and miracles every day and his soul is in heaven.
>
> > His grace in I without blame,
> >   And his soul in Derry,
> > And his dear body under the flagstone
> >   Under which are Bridget and Patrick.

The great stone outside Downpatrick cathedral may still be seen but there is little probability that any of the three saints lie beneath it. In the eighth century Columba's bones were lifted from his grave and laid in a shrine but the monastery was destroyed and its treasures scattered in the Viking raids. Some of his remains were given rest in Dunkeld, which succeeded Iona as the main foundation of the 'parouchia' about 815; other portions of the relics passed to monasteries in Ireland.

The name Iona perpetuates an error, for the 'n' was really 'u' which became inverted, giving a word which in Hebrew means a dove, appropriate as the saint who was to give it fame himself bore the Latin name for the same bird. Ioua is an adjective and the corresponding noun is I or Y, pronounced 'ee' or sometimes Hii, usually coupled to the saint's name in Gaelic, Icolmkill or, more fully, I-chaluimchille. The island is still redolent with memories of the saint and still succeeds in getting across to the materialist of today not a little of the sense of the numinous. This seems in no way due to the Benedictine monks or the Augustine nuns, pious and holy as they may have been, nor to later visitors like Johnson, Boswell or Prince Albert, but solely to the Celtic settlement in and after Columba's day. The mediaeval abbey, in ruins, was given to the Church of Scotland by the 8th Duke of Argyll and restored at the turn of the century; the monastic buildings have been restored since the last war by the Iona Community and will always stand as a great memorial to Lord MacLeod (the Very Rev Dr George MacLeod of Fuinary). Recently parts of the monastic site have been excavated, and these show that (contrary to previous theories) the later abbey was built almost over the monastic settlement.

Columban sites in the western isles and Highlands are distinguished by titles like Clachan Chollumchille (Invermoriston), Eilean Columbkill (Loch Arkaig), Kilcolmkill (Ardnamurchan) and many others.

Other attributions to Columba should be treated with more caution. Kirkcolm in Wigtownshire could be his or some saint called Colm; the island of Inchcolm has a tradition connecting it with the saint, but it is very uncertain. Many modern parishes which had lost sight of their patron have adopted Columba without any historical connection (e.g. St Columba, Dollar), and he has become a popular patron in new housing schemes.

St Columba's Day is 9 June.

An appropriate conclusion to these notes on Columba is his Monastic Rule. Once accepted as the work of Columba himself, it is now thought to date from the time of his successor, Adamnan.

THE RULE OF COLUMCILLE

Be alone in a separate place near a chief city, if thy Conscience is not prepared to be in common with the crowd. Be always naked in imitation of Christ and the Evangelists. Whatsoever little or much thou possesseth of anything, whether clothing, or food or drink, let it be at the command of the senior and at his disposal, for it is not befitting a religious man to have any distinction of property with his own free brother.

Let a fast place with one door enclose thee.

A few religious men to converse with thee of God and his Testament; to visit thee on days of solemnity, to strengthen thee in the Testaments of God and the narratives of the Scriptures.

A person who would talk with thee in idle words or of the world, or who murmurs of what he cannot remedy or but who would distress thee more, should he be a tattler between friends and foes, thou shalt not admit him to thee but at once give him thy benediction should he deserve it.

Let thy servant be a discreet, religious, not tale-telling man, who is to attend continually on thee with moderate labour, of course, but always ready.

Yield submission to every rule that is of devotion.

A mind prepared for red martyrdom.

A mind steadfast and fortified for white maryrdom.

Forgiveness from the heart to everyone.

Constant prayers for those who trouble thee.

Fervour in singing the office for the dead, as if every dead was a particular friend of thine.

Hymn for souls to be sung standing.

Let thy vigils be constant from eve to eve under the direction of another person.

Three labours in the day, viz. prayer, work and reading.

Thy work to be divided into three parts, viz. thine own work and the work of thine place, as regards its real wants; secondly, thy share of the brethren's work; lastly to help the neighbours, viz. by instruction or writing or sewing garments or whatever labour they may be in want of—*ut dominus ait, Non apparebis ante me vacuus.* Everything in its proper order, *Nemo enim, coronabitur nisi nui legitime certaverit.*

Follow almsgiving before all things.

Take not food till thou art hungry.

Sleep not till thou feelest desire.

Speak not except on business.

Every increase which comes to thee in lawful meals or in wearing apparel, give it for pity to the brethren that want it, or to the poor in like manner.

The Love of God with all thy heart and with all thy strength.

The love of thy neighbour as thyself.

Abide in the Testaments of God at all times.
Thy measure of prayer shall be until thy tears come.
Or thy measure of thy work of labour till thy tears come.
Or thy measure of thy work of labour, or of thy genuflexions
until thy perspiration often comes if thy tears are not free.

A. O. and M. O. Anderson (eds), *Adomnan's Life of Columba*, 1961

J. A. Duke, *The Columban Church*, 1931

I. Finlay, *St Columba*, 1979

J. McNeill, *The Celtic Churches*, 1974

comgan

St Comgan (Gaelic pronunciation gives us 'Cowan') was brought up by his father Cellach Cualann, Prince of Leinster, not to be a churchman or a saint but a ruler and warrior. It is probable that in his boyhood an arrow pierced his foot and left him with a limp, but it is possible that this happened during an assassination attempt on his father in the year 715. This was the year when Comgan succeeded to the throne, and we might have prophesied for him many years of power and princely life. Instead, within two years he had voluntarily put it all from him and was crossing the sea to Scotland as one of the 'douloi Christi', the servants of Christ.

In those days spiritual change often implied for the Irish change of all outward associations, including forsaking home and country. Comgan was by no means in the first wave of Irish saints who left their birthland to go 'a-wandering for Christ'. The movement had begun a century and a half earlier and in Comgan's day there were few places left in Scotland or in Europe which had still to hear the gospel for the first time. However, evangelising was a continuing process. As St Patrick had found out so much earlier, once you converted Picts they did not necessarily stay in a 'state of grace' for very long. There would still be plenty of Christian work for Comgan in Scotland, and he took with him his widowed sister, Kentigerna, and her sons.

The obvious place to make for in Scotland would be Luce Bay in Wigtownshire and the most likely beach would be at the Isle of Whithorn, with the old British Christian centre of Candida Casa only a few miles away. It is probable that the party remained here for some time for a significant place-name in the district is the village of Kirkcowan not far away. The party did not settle here, however, perhaps because he found there was little need for his missionary labours; perhaps also because Whithorn was undergoing the most revolutionary changes in its long history. The original Celtic church settlement had decayed (to what extent we cannot now tell), but the bishopric was being revived and brought under the control of Northumbria with an Anglian bishop called Pechthelm. It was now to be ruled from York and taught to look southward to England, and the last shreds of the individualistic and peculiar traits of Celtic Christianity would disappear.

The little party of Irish missionaries moved north. Probably Comgan found it more convenient and more fruitful to choose a district already colonised by fellow Goidheals who spoke his tongue and whose ways he could understand better. He settled at Loch Alsh, where not too far to the north a fellow Irishman, Maelrubha, had been building up an important Christian centre at Applecross. The church at Kirkton Lochalsh, built either by Comgan or by his nephew Fillan became the centre of the parish known thenceforth as Kilchoan. His name is remembered in over half a dozen early sites in the district and his nephew Fillan seems to have worked with him for some time, for Killilans and Kilchoans are grouped near together. Students of the Celtic period of the Church have learned to be extremely cautious of plotting saints' activities by place-names but in these cases there seems no possible explanation other than the presence either of the saint or his disciples.

Comgan's name is traditionally associated with the country east of the Great Glen, particularly at Turriff where, tradition says, he became abbot of the Culdee or Celtic settlement. The parish church there considered him patron, and both St Couan's Hospital and St Couan's Fair denoted his presence.

We have no evidence as to how long he laboured at either centre but the date 734 is suggested by some for the building of his chapel at Turriff on the site where the present parish church stands. Stones with sculpture of the Celtic period have been taken from the church walls, or been found nearby. There is some evidence that the settlement was still there in 1132.

Images of saints were little heard of, if at all, in the early British Church but as time passed they were set up in the churches and great respect was paid to them; usually we know little about them for at the Reformation they were the object of the Reformers' wrath. Comgan's image, a large wooden statue known and reverenced over a wide area of the Highlands as 'the Coan' was taken to Edinburgh at the Reformation and about the year 1600 was burned publicly at the Cross.

Tradition alleges that the saint died at Turriff and his nephew Fillan had the body taken to Iona for burial among the Scottish and Irish royal families.

The festival of Comgan is 13 October, but the year of death is conjectural.

G. A. F. Knight, *Archaeological Light on the Early Christianising of Scotland*, 1933
A. B. Scott, *The Pictish Nation*, 1918

CONAN, patron of Lorne, has left so few traces of his life and work that only with some difficulty can he be distinguished from other saints or missionaries of the same period and very similar names. But no other has a memorial such as Conan has acquired—a modern mini-cathedral in glistening white stone quarried or pulled down from the overhanging Ben Cruachan.

St Conan's, which was only dedicated in 1930, had been planned at the beginning of this century by Walter Campbell, the local proprietor and brother of Lord Blytheswood, who, along with his sister, wanted to give their mother a church which would avoid her having to make the long, difficult walk to Dalmally. Initially the design was a modest one but once Campbell began he replaced his original plans with something much grander. The present St Conan's is the result, a delightful surprise when glimpsed through the trees at the side of perhaps the loveliest of Scottish lochs, Loch Awe. Although Campbell had no architectural training his work has avoided any vulgarism and produced a most modest and seemly place of worship, not unlike an early Christian basilica. The one obvious failing is that it is set in the wilds of very sparsely peopled country and so is likely to pose a perpetual headache to the Church which owns it and has to keep it up.

Even using stone dug from the hillside, the cost when it was built was beyond the means of any but the wealthiest. Its like will never be seen again, but the visitor cannot help wondering if it would have been better to have had it built in a city where it could have filled real need, and been filled with worshippers.

But we have said little about Conan himself. Quite falsely credited with being bishop of Soder and of working in the Isle of Man and the Orkneys, he was one of a large number of Irish missionaries who crossed to the west of Scotland in the seventh century. Firm traces of his work have been obliterated through time, but place-names remain. He is remembered in Angus, sometimes in conjunction with St Vigean. In St Vigean's parish near Arbroath the name Conan occurs several times, e.g. Grange of Conan (an ancient Celtic-type site and chapel), Conansyth Park and Milton of Conan with a hill named Cairn Conan. In Angus he was also known as St Mochonog. In Loch Awe is the island of Inchconain. His fair was formerly held at Glenorchy and at Dalmally there is a St Coonan's Well. His cult was evidently well established in the district.

His festival is 26 January.

G. A. F. Knight, *Archaeological Light on the Early Christianising of Scotland*, 1933

J. C. Martin, *Guidebook to St Conan's Kirk*

CONSTANTINE Take four kings, one saint and a mass of Arthurian and sub-Arthurian legend from areas as far separated as Cornwall and Clydesdale, mix all these well together and see what you get. The result will be very much according to your own fancy—and this is very much what we feel about St Constantine of Govan. One tradition makes him son to Padarn, king of Cornwall (or saint of Wales); another tradition asserts that Arthur himself chose young Constantine to be his successor at the Round Table. Gildas, on the other hand, exposed Constantine's cruelty, especially his murder of the two grandsons of Loth, king of Lothian.

Why Constantine left sunny Cornwall, where he is remembered by the place-names of a bay, a well and a village, is not clear, but we next find him, truly converted as a preaching monk, by the River Clyde. Tradition has it that he was a friend of St Mirren, who had his community at Paisley, and that he decided to set up his own monastery nearby at Govan. Much further up the Clyde valley, where great hills begin to enclose the waters on both banks, Constantine set apart a plot near Crawford where the followers of Christ could meet and where at the end their bones might be laid. The graveyard was named Kirktin Rigg. A few other places in Scotland are rather doubtfully connected with his name, but one, traditionally the scene of his martyrdom, must have mention. Beside Campbeltown Loch, looking over to Davaar Island, is the ruined church of Kilchouslan. There, it is said, a party of pagan robbers came upon the saint and his attendant and hacked them to pieces. His body was recovered, carried down the firth to his monastery at Govan and buried in the sarcophagus, which in 1855 was rescued from long desecration and is now in safe keeping in the parish church.

His festival is 11 March.

G. A. F. Knight, *Archaeological Light on the Early Christianising of Scotland*, 1933

A. G. Williamson, *In the Steps of St Mungo*, 1950

convall

If you feel that God is glorified by breaking His own natural laws and empowering one of His servants to use a stone on which to ride over from Ulster to the River Clyde, then you will feel no doubts about St Convall, who, say the hagiographers (supported strangely enough by such authorities as the great Bishop Forbes), did just this.

Said to have been a colleague of the great Kentigern, Convall traditionally became the evangelist of Renfrew. After crossing from Ulster he landed at Inchinnan, where the Cart joins the Clyde, and worked throughout the district. His stone boat, St Connallie's chariot was to be seen on a nearby hillock where Inchinnan parish church now stands.

There are commemorations to Convall at several places in Ayrshire, and at Huntingtower in Perthshire, all of doubtful antiquity. The most likely centre of his work, if he is really historic, is just where the 'chariot' is said to have landed, not far from a great tyre factory which might give him the right to be taken as patron of pneumatic tyres.

Tradition puts his date of death at 612, and his festival is 28 September.

G. A. F. Knight, *Archaeological Light on the Early Christianising of Scotland*, 1933

curitan or boniface

As we study this saint we must remember that we are dealing neither with Boniface of Canterbury, an arrogant and much disliked prelate, nor with the greatly loved Boniface of Devon, who became the apostle of Germany.

Bede, in his history of the English Church, tells how King Nechtan mac Derile in 710, wishing to convert his Pictish subjects to Roman usage as recommended by the synod of Whitby fifty years earlier, wrote to Abbot Ceolfrid at Wearmouth for guidance on the new customs, and for master-builders to build him a church 'after the Roman style' which he wanted to dedicate to St Peter. From other sources it appears that among those sent to the king was a Pict named Curitan or Kiritinus, who himself had accepted the Roman customs and taken the name of Boniface (Bonifacius).

According to tradition, Curitan returned leading a group of clerics all eager to begin the task of weaning the Picts from their strange schismatic ways to the centralised faith. They sailed up the Tay and landed at the mouth of the little River Gobriat at Invergowrie where they built a church or chapel. The ancient ruin at Dargie, though of course later, occupies the site, while the great Pictish slab with three carved figures (probably Curitan and two other clerics) has been removed to the National Museum of Antiquities in Edinburgh.

Although he had changed his name to Boniface, our saint is still known as Curitan at Invergowrie, and as Celtic missionaries often had 'pet' names it is as St Curdy that he is recognised.

He may next have moved along the Carse to visit King Nechtan at Perth before turning back east along Strathmore to establish Restenneth, which most authorities accept as 'the church after the Roman style', which the king had requested. It received the name of Egglespether, St Peter's church, for Curitan was replacing the Celtic custom of simply naming churches after those who had built them by dedications to Peter as chief of the apostles. Half a century earlier the place had seen the bloodshed of the battle of Nechtansmere close by, when the Picts had defeated the Anglians and slain their king.

The unobtrusive and little known ruin of Restenneth priory, close by Forfar, is one of the most ancient Scottish churches, if not actually the oldest, for the lower courses of the tower probably date from the foundation by Curitan soon after the year 710. Later it became a small priory for Augustinian canons under Jedburgh abbey. King Alexander I had the records from Iona removed here for safety. It was sacked and burnt by the English in the Wars of Independence, fell into ruin at the Reformation but has since been skilfully restored and cared for.

Curitan seems to have remained near Forfar for some time, then moved northwards to settle in the Black Isle at Rosemarkie where he refounded an earlier settlement of St Moluag. Outside Rosemarkie church stands a great Pictish slabstone with symbols both pagan and Christian. In later centuries when local folk economised by using such old monuments as gravestones, they carefully cut it in half so that by turning one part around they could lay it on the ground with only the Christian symbols visible.

His Romanised name of Boniface causes Curitan to be confused too often with continental saints who were also Bonifaces, resulting in such absurd suggestions that he was a Jew who became Pope, but for some reason gave the office up. The *Aberdeen Breviary* gives an incredible and glamorised version of his life, and Hector Boece also 'worked up' his biography. He was of some importance in the Celtic/Roman controversy as he was among the Scottish representatives at the famous synod of Birr (697) along with King Bruide and St Adamnan. Tradition says that Curitan died at Rosemarkie.

He has commemorations both as Curitan and Boniface, e.g. Tobar Churadain (Glen Urquhart), Kilcurdy (Avoch) and Kingoodie (Invergowrie). This last village appears in later records as Kill-curdy. In Inverness-shire there are several Cill- or Tobar- or Cladh-Churadain sites. As Boniface he is linked with St Peter in the cathedral at Fortrose and he also had a chapel at Forfar. Many other Peter dedications are the result of the Curitan mission renaming churches and chapels for the chief apostle: Tealing to St Peter, with a St Peter's well; similarly with Peterculter, Meigle, Fyvie, Peterhead and many others.

At Invergowrie an interesting folk tale concerns the great 'Paddock Stane' which lies in the grounds of and gave its name to what was for long Greystane Hotel, now rechristened. The story is that when the devil saw Curitan's mission coming up the Tay he flung two stones at them. One fell in the river and can be seen as an island; the second fell on land and is the Paddock or Greystane. The story suggests that the devil was concerned that true religion was coming to these parts, but it could also be that he was annoyed that his favourite Celtic Church was being defeated.

One of Curitan's followers on the journey up the Carse of Gowrie was said to be Pesandus, who gave his name to Kilspindie.

J. McNeill, *The Celtic Churches*, 1974
A. Reid, *Picturesque Forfarshire*

CUThbERT The birthplace of Cuthbert

used to be given by scholars as Wrangholm in the Borders but now objections have been raised to this so we shall leave the place uncertain but put the date as 634. He lived through two major historical events. The first was a major visitation of the yellow plague which crossed from Europe and swept up through England, reducing the population by up to half and leaving the monasteries bereft of many of their leaders and thousands of their monks and lay-brothers. Cuthbert caught the infection but was fortunate enough to recover even with, apparently, a slight deformity. Second, in 664 came the famous synod of Whitby where the conflicting claims of the Roman and Celtic rites were decided in favour of the former.

As we are employing the term 'Celtic' Church in these pages it may be an appropriate point to explain the meaning. Since the withdrawal of the Roman legions at the beginning of the fifth century, communications with the continental Church became less and less possible and so both British and Irish Churches largely went their own way. The remarkable fact was that they seemed to differ very little in doctrine from the main continental stream, but in government, and on some points of practice, they did differ. The kind of monks' tonsure, the form of the blessing and minor variations of liturgy cannot have worried either side greatly; the date on which Easter was celebrated did so, partly because it was awkward if one group was fasting while others were celebrating, and also because any practice which broke rigid uniformity was distasteful to the 'catholic' or 'Roman' party. The underlying difference which was proving impossible to solve was the framework of Church government. Celtic Christianity centred wholly round monasteries each under the control of an abbot, and the function of the bishops who were attached to each monastery was relatively minor, mainly ordaining new monks as priests. In the continental Church, the English Church as established by Augustine and other 'catholic' areas, countries were divided into dioceses, each under a bishop who had monarchical powers and who alone decided doctrine. Only in bishops did the fulness of the ministry repose.

Conflict came to a head at several points but more publicly and most noticeably in the Northumbrian Church. At Whitby the debate was argued out and the Roman view prevailed. Increasing pressure was henceforth applied to abbots and monks to discard what were now being called their 'heresies', although in doctrine there was no difference between them.

Cuthbert spent the first part of his ministry within the Celtic type of monastery. Bede wrote a little history of Cuthbert's life in which he recounts a vision Cuthbert had when acting as shepherd on the Lammermuir Hills on the night Aidan died at Bamburgh. As a result of this vision the youth presented himself to Boisel, the prior of Old Maelros (a daughter community of Lindisfarne). Bede says of young Cuthbert: 'He loved games and pranks and loved to play with other children. He was naturally agile and quick-witted and usually won the game.' It seems, however, that when a lad he developed some form of tuberculosis (or perhaps it was a result of the plague): 'his knee suddenly began to hurt and a great tumour swelled up causing the muscles of the knee-cap to contract.' It was healed at the time but is mentioned again later and it is said that when at the end of last century the body of Cuthbert was examined at Durham there were signs that the bones had for some time suffered tuberculosis.

Some of the stories of the saint recounted by Bede show Cuthbert wandering through the Borders on his monastic duties and evangelistic campaigns. One Friday, on a long, lonely trip, a woman at a cottage offered him food, which he refused as it was a fast day. She warned him, 'You will not find another village on your way, nor even a house and it will take you till sunset to reach your destination. At least take something with you or you will be fasting the whole day, perhaps even until tomorrow.' The saint refused, but as he journeyed he found how true the woman's words had been. Late next night, quite exhausted, he at last found some shepherds' huts, used for the summer but now deserted. His horse, as hungry as he was, started to pull straw out of the thatched roof to eat and dislodged a parcel wrapped in linen; the shepherds had left some food which the saint thankfully took, exclaiming, 'O God, I was fasting for the love of Thee and in return Thou hast fed both me and my animal. Blessed be Thy name!'

This is only one of many tales of Cuthbert's love of animals. 'We have to wait till St Godric appears in the twelfth century,' writes James Brodrick, 'to meet another saint who had so much sympathy with the birds and beasts and all wild sentient things of nature.'

With his abbot Eata, Cuthbert was sent to the monastery of Ripon but when the king joined the Romanising party all the Scots monks were driven out and he went back to Melrose. After the synod of Whitby Cuthbert obediently adopted the new ways and indeed became enthusiastic in enforcing new usages at Lindisfarne where he was appointed prior under Eata. Within, however, he was unhappy. So many evidences of the Church conflict were all around him—the saintly Colman had been head of this family but now, driven almost into exile, was spending his last years away on the west coast of Ireland.

On Lindisfarne Cuthbert withdrew to the tiny islet now known as St Cuthbert's Island where we may still trace outlines of his oratory and feel his presence very real. After twelve years he left and crossed to the more remote Farne Islands where he adopted the complete hermit's life, erecting a cell with such high walls that he could see only the sky and the ocean. It is difficult to admire him away there. 'He kept his soft leather boots on his feet for months on end without removing them,' writes Bede and we cannot help being glad that after nine years of such seclusion he was, with great difficulty, compelled by the Church authorities to return to the world, accepting the bishopric of Lindisfarne. On Easter Day, 685, Cuthbert was consecrated at York by Archbishop Theodore in presence of the king. The era of the abbot and the Celtic tonsure were dead; Cuthbert was now symbolic of the new Church, with all the pomp and pageantry. He was now a monarchical bishop.

Cuthbert had little time left but he made the most of it. In 685 there was a notable visit to Carlisle after he was appointed to his see. He inspected what was left of the old Roman city, established the church whose successor still holds him as patron, and founded a school which only fairly recently has been liquidated by modern educational policy. He also spoke with the queen about her decision to take the nun's habit following the death of her king at Nechtansmere in Angus, and he chatted with St Herbert who had journeyed from his Derwentwater retreat to bid farewell to him.

In 687, in failing health, he withdrew to his old retreat on the Farnes. On 20 March a light shone across the water, the signal by which the monks on Lindisfarne would know their bishop had entered into rest.

One of the most remarkable stories in history concerns Cuthbert's body. Originally kept at Lindisfarne, after some years it was found uncorrupted. Two centuries later, when the island fell before the attacks of Danes, the monks took the coffin and fled, carrying with them both it and the beautiful manuscript known as the Lindisfarne Gospels. Their boat was wrecked off Cumbria while they were trying to reach Ireland, but the book in its case was recovered unharmed. For a century the coffin rested in the church of Chester-le-Street, but fear of another Viking invasion caused its guardians, successors to the first monks who had set out with it from Lindisfarne, to bear it on to Ripon and finally to Durham. When in 1827 the coffin was opened for the last time the vestments and the little pastoral cross were still in it. Cross and coffin—still wonderfully preserved and carved with symbols of the evangelists—lie in the library of Durham university.

In Scotland, Kirkcudbright, of course, is Cuthbert's town and chapels, wells, fairs etc to him are too numerous to mention. Many, of course, are probably much later than the saint's date but others were probably memories of where the coffin had rested on its long journey. The West Kirk of Edinburgh has undoubted early associations with Cuthbert. Elsewhere the name is sometimes found in its 'pet' form—St Cuddie.

Border parishes are studded with Cuthbert place-names.

His festival is 20 March.

A. O. and M. O. Anderson (eds), *Adomnan's Life of Columba,* 1961

B. Colgrave and R. A. B. Mynors (eds), *Bede: Historia Ecclesiastica,* 1969

H. Mayr-Harting, *The Coming of Christianity,* 1972

K. Parbury, *The Saints of Lindisfarne,* 1970

CYRUS

CYRUS It is in this form that the child martyr is known in the east-coast fishing village of which he is patron. He was a Roman martyr of the early fourth century, son of Julitta who after severe torture was beheaded while the child, reputedly only three years old, had his brains dashed out. His cult, which recognised him as the intercessor for children in trouble, spread rapidly.

There are several variations on his name—Cyrcus, Cyricius and (strangely) St Greg, which was the older name of the village, Ecclesgreg.

Forbes, in his kalendar, admits to being somewhat uncertain if the saint of Ecclesgreg is the same youthful martyr, but we know his cult was observed in Scotland and his name appears in the Pictish Chronicle. He may be the patron saint of the Fife town of Ceres.

His festival is 16 June.

D. H. Farmer, *Oxford Dictionary of Saints,* 1978

A. P. Forbes, *Kalendars of Scottish Saints,* 1872

David I We tend to treat royal saints with caution and perhaps not a little suspicion, wondering if courtly influence and worldly prestige had not played a part and influenced their canonisation. Certainly some very doubtful monarchs appeared in the saintly kalendars, including the worldly Malcolm, husband to the saintly Margaret of Scotland. Of David I, however, there can be little doubt about his religious devotion, his enthusiasm for the welfare of the Church and his generosity in providing for the temporal needs of abbeys and cathedrals. So we should allow his place in the kalendar although as a monarch he did adopt some very bloodthirsty tactics. He surely must have had a great questioning of conscience when he found himself engaged against the banners of a whole battery of saints—Peter, Cuthbert, Wilfred and John of Beverley among others. In less troubled times, however, others, with much less excuse, have shed much blood in the name of the Prince of Peace.

At the end of a long life, David was taken ill at Carlisle, at that time within his own domains. He was found by his attendant—dead and at prayer. He was buried in Dunfermline.

His festival is 24 May.

H. Fenwick, *Scottish Abbeys and Cathedrals*, 1978
R. Masson, *Scotland: The Nation*, 1934

david of wales

When Scots folk talk of St David more often than not they mean the patron of Wales, Dewi Sant, rather than King David, son of Queen Margaret. Dewi Ddyfrwr, David the water drinker, was roughly contemporary with Columba but he lacked a biographer like Adamnan to record his life and works. Rhygyfarch (1057–99) came so much later that his Latin *Life of St David,* alleges Professor Bowen, 'cannot be relied on for a single historical fact'.

Tradition obligingly furnished the saint with a princely pedigree—son of a Welsh chief named Sant, great-grandson of Cunedda Wledig, the famous prince who led his people south from Scotland to help the Welsh Britons to repel Irish invaders. His mother was Nonnita, also reputedly the daughter of a chief, although another suggestion says that she was a nun raped by the prince.

David was born on the Cardigan coast at a place called Mynyw, Latinised to Menevia, now Henfynw. When he set up a community he chose a place further south on a neck of land, the Vallis Rosina or Valley of the Little Bog. Later, in his honour, it was known as Ty Ddewi, David's House, and it is now the miniature cathedral city of St. David's. Later, when Canterbury achieved control of the Welsh Church, history was distorted to present David as the first diocesan bishop of south-west Wales corresponding to St Dubricius at Llandaf in the south-east. Diocesan or monarchical bishops came to the British Church much later than David's time and we should picture the ancient Ty Ddewi as the simple cultic centre of a very large number of daughter communities, the 'family' or

68

'parouchia' of the saint. David probably represented a 'puritan' element in the early British
Church which led to his nickname of 'Waterman'
and his monastic rules were probably more
severe than those imposed in other monasteries.

Bowen has plotted the sites of some two score
Dewi 'cills' or churches in south-west Wales, a
smaller cluster in Gwent and over into Hereford,
and several separated foundations in Cornwall,
Devon and Brittany, but there is no record of a
single ancient foundation honouring David any
further north. Only by courtesy, therefore, could
he be considered patron of all Wales; and even in
the south, saints such as Teilo or Padarn would
have equal right to the honour.

In addition to the Scottish link if the saint's
descent from the chieftain, Cunedda Wledig, be
accepted, Dr A. B. Scott suggested that David
had been educated at Candida Casa—an attractive possibility but without any obvious historical
foundation. In the west of Scotland there are
several ancient dedications, introducing forms
such as Kildavie (Southend); Weem (Perthshire)
has a David as patron, and there is a Cladh-cill-
Dabhi (rock of David's chapel), a Davie's fair, a
Kildave and a Dundavie near Aberfeldy. Kippen-
davie is near Dunblane and there are other
similar dedications. It is unlikely, however, that
these have a connection with the Welsh saint. It
has been suggested (by Frank Knight and others)
that they derive from St Dabius, a follower of St
Patrick. Dewi Sant's emblem is not a leek or a
daffodil but is in fact a dove.

His festival is 1 March.

E. G. Bowen, *Settlements of the Celtic Saints in Wales*, 1955
A. W. Wade-Evans, *Welsh Christian Origins*, 1934

devenick

The name does not appear in the usual lists of Irish Celtic missionary saints and very little is known about him although the small community and the parish of Banchory-Devenick bear his name. Bishop Forbes places him in the period of the Columban mission while Knight thinks he was fifth century. All agree that his sphere was north-east Scotland, especially the valleys of the Don and the Aberdeenshire Dee. The *Aberdeen Breviary* claims that his body was buried at the place later called after him. 'Criech,' writes Forbes, 'was probably dedicated to this saint, known there as Teavneck.' Methleck has a Devenick's Well and once held a fair in his honour.

His festival is 13 November.

G. A. F. Knight, *Archaeological Light on the Early Christianising of Scotland*, 1933

donan

A remarkable fact about the widespread work of the Celtic missionary saints from the fifth century onwards is that scarcely any cases of violent opposition or martyrdom are recorded until the Viking and Danish raids began at the end of the ninth century. The pagan Celts accepted the missionaries even when they did not accept their religion and pagan and Christian symbols are found side by side on the great pictish stones.

Donan (or Donnan) deserves a note in these pages not only because of the extent of his journeyings but because he and his fellow monks on the island of Eigg provide the most dreadful case of martyrdom in the history of the Celtic Church. He and fifty-two of his followers were butchered within the refectory of the monastery. The only other martyrdoms recorded seem to be those of Constantine of Kintyre and of Kessog, and the latter is doubtful.

Unfortunately the mediaeval *Life* of Donan is lost, and what little we know of him is limited to the brief comments in such ancient martyrologies as Tallaght, Donegal and Oengus. The date of his birth is not known but he was contemporary with, or a little younger, than Columba. We presume that he was Irish and early in adult life crossed to Galloway. Thereafter we only know him through a chain of Kildonans up the west coast of Scotland, beginning with a Kildonan at Kirkmaiden and a Chapel Donan at Kirkcolm, and terminating at Kildonan on the island of Little Bernera in the Outer Hebrides.

The story of Donan's martyrdom was by no means unknown in mediaeval Scotland and some commemorations might be due to later interest and veneration. But the plotting of the place-names suggests a logical route of missionary progression northwards. The only St Donnan's east of the Great Glen is at Auchterless in Aberdeenshire, and it has been suggested that Donan had a special connection with this parish—there are several place-names and we know his 'bachail' or staff was kept there till the Reformation. Perhaps for this very reason the saint's personal connection with Auchterless is more open to doubt, as the possession of the bachail in mediaeval days might well lead to the name instead of vice versa.

Only one incident is recorded as happening during these missionary years. He crossed to Iona to meet Columba, and according to the story, asked that saint to act as his 'anamchara' or 'soul-friend', which took the place of the

Roman Church's 'confessor'. Strangely enough, Columba refused to act as anamchara, saying, 'I shall not be a soul-friend to a company of red-martyrdom.' Obviously some explanation must be sought for this abrupt refusal. Dr A. B. Scott, who disliked Columba, saw in it the Goidheal's refusal to have any friendly intercourse with a Pict, but there could be quite different reasons, such as Columba's unwillingness to accept the additional responsibility which the duty entailed.

Donan eventually formed his community on the small island of Eigg, with the monastic buildings on the side facing Arisaig. It had become a large community by the date of the massacre—fifty-two is the number of monks given in the record, although for some unknown reason only fifty names are listed. It has been suggested that the monks are fictional but Dr Scott was sure he had traced local place-names deriving from them. Did Donan cross from Ireland with the nucleus of such a group ready formed? Did he start with one or two and build to over fifty? Any answer to such questions would be as vague as the reason for the sudden unprecedented attack. On this subject scholars have made much of an obscure statement in the martyrologies that the monks' keeping sheep on the island had angered a local woman of importance. Scott draws the unwarranted conclusion that when the local folk refused to take action she deliberately bribed a group of pirates to make the attack. It cannot, of course, be proved that she did not do so, so the reason for the brutality must remain conjectural. Pirates were by no means unknown but it is doubtful that they would take time to raid an obscure, penniless and inoffensive group of monks. It is more likely to have been a very early group of 'Black Gentiles' from Jutland or Denmark.

Details of the raid differ. Donan, it is said, was celebrating the Sacrament when the intruders broke in. When he begged for respite till mass was completed, they agreed and he led the monks across to the refectory 'that the place where God had been worshipped in spiritual joy might not be polluted with their blood'. The *Martyrology of Donegal* then states that 'he was beheaded and 52 of the monks with him' while that of Oengus suggests that the building was set on fire and they all perished in the flames. The traditional year of the massacre was 618.

Dr Simpson in his book provides a map or track-chart of suggested Donan foundations. Almost all are forms of Kildonan—on Skye, Little Bernera, Uist and, on the mainland, Little Loch Broom, Kishorn (Seipeil Dhonnain), Eilean Dhonnain, Cil Dhonnain (Loch Garry) and St Donnan's (Auchterless). In the south we find Kildonans at Arran, Kintyre (now wrongly called Kildonald), Colmonell, Kirkmaiden and Chapel Donnan in Kirkcolm.

Donan's festival is 16 or 17 April.

A. B. Scott, *The Pictish Nation*, 1918
W. D. Simpson, *The Celtic Church in Scotland*, 1935

drostan This saint has caused much controversy among scholars. One of the mediaeval manuscripts, the *Book of Deer* in Cambridge university library, written about the ninth century, contains in its margins, written about two centuries later, an account of the reputed founding of the religious settlement at Deer in Aberdeenshire. It claims that Columba, with his nephew Drostan, landed at Aberdour, near Fraserburgh and, after founding a monastery, they moved inland. After some difficulty, they secured land for a second foundation. Columba gave this land to Drostan who burst into tears, at which his uncle cried 'Let Dear be its name'. This is a silly pun on the Gaelic 'deur' for 'tear' and must be dismissed as nonsense, but it has caused scholars to question the whole story. There is no record of Columba having a nephew Drostan; indeed, the name is not Gaidhealic but Brythonic or Pictish, and the foundation was probably a generation before Columba's time. When north Britain was unified under the Scots there were important influences stressing its Gaidhealic origins and minimising the contributions of the Pictish and Brythonic elements. Not only may this account for this false account of the origin of Deer but it led to Scott and others maintaining that many lives of the Celtic saints had been tampered with in order to magnify the Columban Church against the Pictish missionaries. The controversy continues today.

Dr G. A. F. Knight stresses a comment in the *Martyrology of Oengus* which mentions 'Drostan and his three'. This is interpreted as meaning Drostan with Colm, Medan and Fergus. Nothing is known of the lives of any of these figures except that they all left a great many place-names in Aberdeenshire and the north-east.

Drostan's name appears on the famous stone in the St Vigean's museum. It is on a small panel at the side and seems to read:

Dorsten ipe voret ett Forcvs.

There are as many interpretations of the meaning of this as there are letters in the inscription, ranging from the simple 'Drosten, Ipevoret and Forcus' to 'O Cross, time will destroy thee, too'. One modern authority doubts if it means anything and there is increasing suspicion that the lettering was no part of the original memorial. Some believe Drostan to be a variant of Tristan, which would bring the saint into the orbit of the Arthurian legends.

Drostan, or some namesake of his, has several place-names in Galloway. In Anwoth parish is Trusty's Hill which possesses one of the few Pictish symbols found south of the Forth and in the same area we find Bardreston, Bardriston and Bardrostan. Drostan is also found as St Modrustus at Markinch (Fife) where he was patron of the mediaeval church. In Glenesk (Angus) is the Kirk of Droustie. His name has always been associated with Deer where in mediaeval times the church was dedicated to 'Christ, Peter, Columcille and Drostan'. A local fair was St Dustan's. In some places he is St Dunstan. Insch (Aberdeenshire) has always considered him patron, as has Urquhart (Inverness-shire) which was known as St Drostan's Urquhart to distinguish it from a similarly named parish further north. It is also possible that Beauly priory originally held him as patron.

His festival is 11 July.

G. A. F. Knight, *Archaeological Light on the Early Christianising of Scotland*, 1933
A. B. Scott, *The Pictish Nation*, 1918
W. D. Simpson, *The Celtic Church in Scotland*, 1935

duꞇhac Coming on the scene at the end of the Celtic period when Roman customs had been very generally adopted, Duthac's life-span

witnessed also the Viking invasions in their full fury. He was born in Tain, Easter Ross, traditionally at a spot below the town where a chapel dedicated to him still stands, although now in ruins. Duthac's learning and piety soon became recognised as outstanding; Irish chronicles hailed him as 'Primus anamchara, Praecipius confessarius'. At one stage, he is said to have crossed to Ireland for further study, and later he returned to Ireland and died at Armagh in 1065.

Of his work in Tain and its neighbourhood not a single incident or anecdote survives except those connected with the remarkable cures attributed to him. It is quite impossible to reconstruct his biography, but it must have been full of interest for his reputation is still strong in the county and beyond. The position he held in the Church is not known. It was later accepted that he had been bishop but this may have been in the Celtic, prediocesan sense.

Duthac was popularly recognised as a saint long before there was any formal process of canonisation. It was Archibald, Earl of Douglas, who drew attention to his suitability for canonisation, claiming this to be the wish of the entire Scottish people. Duthac survived the formal inquisition, many miracles were cited and his name was added to the Roman Kalendar at 8 March.

The great Bishop Elphinstone, for a brief period bishop at Ross before going on to Aberdeen, made a selection from Scottish and Irish sources of miracles attributed to Duthac and printed them in the *Aberdeen Breviary*. An early miracle attributed to young Duthac happened when he was sent to the smithy for some fire. For some reason the smith gathered hot coals on a shovel and flung them at the boy. Duthac calmly gathered them in his apron and returned un-scathed to his master. Another story describes Duthac taking part in a feast when a guest falls sick and a hungry kite flies away with both the uneaten food and a gold ring. Duthac prays and the bird returns to bring back the stolen food. Duthac keeps the ring but gives the bird the food.

The high reputation of the saint ensured that Tain would not become a forgotten parish. Translation of his body from Armagh back to Tain was recorded in 1253, and the town long treasured his relics, including a shirt which protected the wearer from injury or death. When the Earl of Ross was killed at Halidon Hill while wearing the shirt, the English returned it to the Scots. The ancient chapel of Duthac which is little altered must be early, perhaps before 1100, for it is not orientated as is the later church.

Loch Duich takes its name from Duthac. There is a suppressed parish of Balmaduthie at Knock-bain. Newburgh was originally Duthacs. At Wick, folk used to take food and silver to the ancient St Dudoch's kirk. James IV made his pilgrimage to the shrine in 1505.

A. P. Forbes, *Kalendars of Scottish Saints*. 1872

Ebba

St Abb's upon the Nabbs,
 St Helen's upon the Lea,
St Bee's upon Dunbar Sands
 Stands closest to the sea.

This ancient snatch of Northumbrian folk-rhyme attributes the foundation of three Anglo-Saxon monasteries or nunneries to the wreck of a ship-load of princesses off the Dunbar coast after which each set out to found her own community. If there is any truth in this story all traces of Helen's (at Cockburnspath) and St Bee's at Dunbar have long since disappeared. Ebba's convent on the Nabbs at Coldingham, however, grew to become an important coeducational monastery of the Celtic type, of which some few traces remain today.

Ebba, Aebba, or Abba was in no sense merely a legend but very much an historical figure; the daughter of King Aethelfrith of Bernicia, sister of the princes Eanfrith, Oswald and Oswy. On the death of King Edwin at the hands of Cadwallon, Aethelfrith's children, three boys and the young girl Ebba, felt it was safe to return to Northumbria from Iona where they had spent most of their childhood in exile. It is a relief to turn from the bloodstained story of the Anglian kings to the peace of Iona where this party of royal refugees played on the sands, roamed the Machar, wondered at the sight of the spouting cave, and, let us hope, forgot for a while that soon they would

78

have to face the responsibilities of royalty. When news came of their enemy Edwin's death, preparations were made for the return to the palace at Bamburgh where the eldest boy would have to claim the throne. It is said that considerable pressure was put on Ebba to marry the Scots heir but to this she replied that the idea of any husband was repulsive as she had pledged herself to perpetual virginity. Strangely, her brothers did not force the issue, as in those days they might well have done.

Allowed to go her own way Ebba found a secluded place north-west of Durham on the site of the long deserted Roman fort of Vindomara and established a monastery where in a deep glen a little burn joins the River Derwent. In this quiet place the Christian daughter of that fierce pagan known as the 'ravening wolf' might have lived for the rest of her life, but for some reason she moved on and re-established her community on a rocky headland near Coldingham, some miles north of the royal city of Bamburgh. Maybe in her sheltered inland monastery at Ebchester she had missed the challenge of the sea and rocks she had known in Iona.

About the quality of her personal life and the purity of her motives there was never any question, but of the discipline in the convent two authorities, Bede himself and, later, Capgrave, both speak in terms of severe disapproval. Indeed, Bede's summing up makes it seem more like a hippy commune than a sober and godly Anglo-Saxon community.

nam et domunculae, quae ad orandum vel legendum factae erant, nunc in commessationum, popationum fabulationum sunt illecebrarum cubilia conversae.

apartments built for prayer or reading are now turned into places for feasting, drinking, gossiping and frivolity.

Bede claims as authority for his comments a priest called Adamnan (not Columba's biographer) who had been attached to the monastery. As the result of a vision in which he foresaw the destruction of the community he told the abbess Ebba exactly what was going on. 'Why did you not tell me this before?' was her naive reply and as a result, writes Bede, 'The community was somewhat alarmed for a few days', as well it might have been—and it began to abandon sinfulness and do penance.

Soon after Ebba's death, however, conduct again deteriorated and before the time that Bede was writing the foretold destruction took place. The monk accuser claimed that a fellow monk at Jarrow, formerly at St Abb's, had witnessed these events. In spite of all this, Cuthbert loved the place and used to spend whole nights down on the shore, but it was said that it was the scandal at St Abb's which caused him to develop the anti-feminist sentiments for which he was later to be noted.

We may doubt if things at Ebba's monastery were ever as bad as Bede painted them. He was no lover of the Celtic institutions and their freer attitude to mixed monasteries would prejudice a defender of the strict Roman separation of men and women against St Abb's. But Bede refers to Ebba herself as 'a pious woman and a handmaid of Christ'. Queen Ethelthryth, former wife of Ecgfrith, Ebba's uncle, was for a year a novice at St Abb's before she went on to found her own community at Ely, and if she knew of scandal she kept it to herself.

Ebba died in 683. The burning of her monastery which had been forecast occurred soon afterwards. Her festival is on 25 August but on 2 April there is a second Ebba festival. The story behind this is dealt with under the saint whom we have called Ebba the Second.

B. Colgrave and R. A. B. Mynors (eds), *Bede: Historia Ecclesiastica*, 1967

ebba the second

This holy lady is often regarded merely as a literary-historical 'doublet', a late mirror image of the real Ebba of St Abb's. Such doublets are suspected in scriptural and historical incidents and consist of a story, originally a single incident, becoming twisted through being told so often. Eventually the story is accepted as two distinct incidents, differing in some minor features. In the gospels, scholars have for long suggested that the Feeding of the Four Thousand is a doublet of the similar miracle involving Five Thousand. In our case, the first Ebba of the seventh century is well documented. She frequently appears in Bede's narratives and is undoubtedly a real abbess who died on or about 683.

The second Ebba is a lot less definite, but she does seem worthy of a separate entry among our saints. There is a lively Northumbrian tradition, backed by documents now unfortunately lost, of an abbess of Coldingham named Ebba being brutally murdered, along with her nuns, by the Danes in 874. There was at Coldingham a separate festival, 2 April, in her honour.

One can see the possibility of this story being a doublet when the original Ebba had become almost forgotten along with all the details of the seventh-century incident—the invading Danes are introduced and the gruesome ending added. On the other hand we know of instances in Celtic monasteries where a later abbot or abbess took the name of an illustrious predecessor, and the dates do fit well with a Danish raid.

The only recorded incident connected with this second Ebba is the dreadful story of the Danes. Warned of their approach and of their record of rape and massacre the abbess cut open her nose and lips with a razor and commanded her nuns (for the community was by then, of course, single sex) to follow her example. The Danes, it was said, were so disgusted at the sight that they retreated, but later returned, burnt the buildings and murdered the women. This story is so dreadful, even for those days, that one hopes it has become exaggerated through the years. The year of this massacre, writes Forbes, was 874. The monastery at Coldingham was rebuilt in 1088.

D. H. Farmer, *Oxford Dictionary of Saints*, 1978
A. P. Forbes, *Kalendars of Scottish Saints*, 1872

edwin
Geographically, Edwin, the king of Northumbria, has every right to appear in a book of Scottish saints, for at that time Northumbria was by no means just Northumberland, but took in the Lothians, including Edinburgh. Whether spiritually he had a right to the title 'saint' is another matter which we will not argue over. In sheer bloodthirstiness there was little to chose between pagan and Christian monarchs in those days, and there was constant court intrigue and assassination of monarchs. Edwin himself was a refugee in East Anglia in childhood and when he came to power it was the turn of the family of his rival Ethelfrith to flee for their lives.

The Christian chroniclers, however, especially Bede, speak highly of Edwin, his gentleness and the wide peace he brought to his kingdom. Edwin took time and gave much thought to his religious position and at last in York on Easter 627 the king was baptised. Already the queen's chaplain, Paulinus, had held a great mass baptism of Edwin's subjects in the tiny River Glen which lies today on the very boundary between England and Scotland and where at Yeavering Bell the king had his great palace of Gefrin.

Although Edwin's right to rule Lothian was not seriously challenged, he does not seem to have made use of Edinburgh, which, it is now recognised, is not named after him, but was perhaps derived from Dunedin which seems to mean 'the fort on a slope'. Walter Scott took it as the site of the ancient Dinas Eiddyn. This, however, is likely to refer to a hill in north Wales. An early name for the place was Castrum Puellarum, Maiden Castle, which may go very many centuries beyond the saint Modwenna of the sixth century, who sometimes gets credit for this title.

Edwin himself fell, like almost all his contemporaries, at the hands of his enemies. In 633 at Hatfield Chase he was slain by Cadwallon of Wales and Penda of Mercia who had together invaded Northumbria.

His festival is 12 October.

P. Hunter Blair, *Roman Britain and Early England*, 1963

enoch is the more popular name for Thenew, who was also known as Denw and as Thanay. She was traditionally the daughter of King Loth or Leudonus of Lothian and mother of

Kentigern. Wooed by Owain or Ewen, son of Urien, one of the great Brythonic heroes, she was found to be pregnant. There are several versions of the incident, some suggesting a virgin birth, which was rejected as sacrilegious; others held that Ewen had disguised himself as a maiden to deceive her; in other suggestions a mysterious swine-herd is the father. It is obvious that the variants are all attempts to preserve the honour of the princess. Her father, however, was not satisfied and decreed that she must die, but whether for unchastity or because she had preferred the swine-herd to the prince is not made clear.

An attempt to send her hurtling down Dunpelder (Traprain Law) in a chariot was unsuccessful when the shafts caught in the rocks where you may see the scrape-marks (glaciation, probably) today. She was then cast off in an open boat from Aberlessic (possibly Aberlady or Tyninghame). The craft floated out past May Island but was supported by a great shoal of fish and carried up the Forth to land at Culross just as the baby was born.

The whole story savours more of myth or legend than history and may have risen from a tradition which refused to be suppressed that Kentigern was illegitimate. Being cast off in an open boat is a well known Celtic myth with psychological overtones and is told also about Blane, Maccoul and others.

Enoch was apparently not a Christian at this time for when the aged Serf took charge of the refugees who had been washed up on the shore near his settlement he hurried to baptise both mother and child. His words when told of their coming, recorded in the Herbertian *Life of Kentigern*, were, 'A Dia cur fir sin', 'O God, may this be true'. This is a rather poor attempt to explain the word 'Kentigern' which must mean something like 'Lord of the hounds'. Serf continued to care for the boy and his mother and gave him the nick-name of Mungo, 'little doggie', as the baby followed him like a puppy.

We have no details of Enoch's life. She evidently moved to Glasgow where her son founded his community and on her death she was buried where the later parish church of St Enoch stood, by the place where the Molendinar Burn flows into the Clyde. Modern Glaswegians know her best by the railway station and the busy square which bear her name.

Welsh tradition recognises the saint as Dwynwen, daughter of Llewddyn Lueddog of Dinas Eiddyn.

Her festival is 18 July.

K. H. Jackson, *Studies in the Early British Church*, 1958

FERGUS

FERGUS The little Aberdeenshire village of St Fergus, honouring in its title an early Pictish missionary, has recently achieved fame through the bringing to shore of North Sea oil and gas. On its links near the sea, east of the present church, is an ancient graveyard with traces of a chapel which may be the successor to a mud and wattle 'cil' built by the saint for missionary work in this remote district.

The life of Fergus has to be reassembled from various clues, for the account in the *Book of Deer*, which depicts him as nephew to St Columba, has all the appearance of a mediaeval attempt to elevate Iona and Gaidhealic influence on parts of Scotland which had been by race and culture Pictish. Place-names, if they are used with proper caution, provide clues for the activities of these early missionaries. Fergus was obviously held in great honour in the north-east, and the number of dedications to him suggest that this area was the centre of his work. The same district contains similar indications of the cult of three other Pictish saints—Drostan, Medan and Colm. Their tracks seem to cross and recross so frequently that we may suspect a missionary team evangelising the north-east, perhaps about the beginning of the sixth century. The Irish *Martyrology of Oengus,* dating probably from the ninth century but fairly reliable as a guide to the saints, writes of 'Trursus cona thriur'—'Drostan with his three'—for Thursus is usually accepted as Tristram or Drostan. This would suggest Drostan as the leader and his community at Deer (later to become a great mediaeval monastery) as the 'beancor' or missionary centre, serving the north-east as Applecross served the north-west, Iona the Gaidhealic, Argyll and Whithorn the south-west.

While it is attractive to picture Fergus working along with Drostan, Medan and Colm in a first wave of Christian evangelisation even before Columba began his activities in the west, it has been suggested by Dr Skene and others that he belonged to the following century and is to be identified with Fergustus, a Pictish bishop who attended a council at Rome in 721. If this later date be accepted it would not detract from the importance of his missionary activities in north-east Scotland.

He is recognised as patron of Wick, the seal of which former burgh showed the saint in an open boat with two rowers. Legend asserts that he produced calm in the midst of a storm by casting his staff into the sea. Until the year 1613 the burgh of Wick is said to have possessed a stone image of the saint to which its citizens were so attached that when the local minister, in a burst of anti-superstitious enthusiasm, had it destroyed, they threw him into the river and drowned him. Obviously there is some doubt about this tradition, and still more about the version that asserts that the saint himself took a hand in the affair and was seen mounted on the minister's back holding his head under water.

Previous to the Reformation, Aberdeen cathedral recorded possession of a 'silver arm of St Fergus with his bones'. This would be a reliquary similar to the 'Shrine of St Patrick's Hand' in the National Museum of Ireland. It had been gifted to the cathedral by the rector of Dyce where the saint was honoured as patron of the parish whose original title was Chapel of St Fergus. By tradition Fergus died and was buried at Glamis which, like its neighbours Eassie and Nevay, had Fergus as Patron. The body remained at Glamis but the head was taken to the monastery at Scone where a silver case was made for it by James IV.

Fergus is a Brythonic or Pictish name and the area covered by dedications to him coincides almost exactly with the area of the great Pictish inscribed stones, both those with purely pagan symbols and those bearing also representations of the cross.

Fergus was also commemorated at Chapelmill (Montrose), Pethergus (Kincardineshire), Fetterangus (Aberdeenshire), Halkirk (Caithness) and Moy (Inverness-shire). Loch Fergus (Wigtownshire) might possibly suggest that he was educated at nearby Candida Casa. Finally, the Catholic church and school at Adler, Dundee, are dedicated to St Fergus.

Fergus is commemorated in the kalendar of the Scottish Episcopal Church on 15 November, although tradition puts his festival date at 27 November.

An early and quite distinct Fergus, this one from Carnock near Airth, comes into the story of Kentigern. When Kentigern left Culross and moved west he found the aged Fergus dying, and took him on an ox-cart to find a burial place. The oxen halted at Cathures, a place taken to be Glasgow, and Fergus was buried in the cemetery consecrated long before by Ninian. Traditionally, therefore, Fergus was the first to lie in the crypt of

Glasgow cathedral. The historicity of this Fergus incident is doubted by many scholars.

A. P. Forbes, *Kalendars of Scottish Saints*, 1872
G. A. F. Knight, *Archaeological Light on the Early Christianising of Scotland*, 1933

fillan

St Fillan's blessed well,
 Whose spring can frenzied dreams dispel
 And the crazed brain restore.

Walter Scott's verse rings false to this particular modern hagiographer who spends long hours in libraries endeavouring to disentangle the lives of various 'Fillans' or 'Faolans' who wandered our country in the days of the Celtic Church. My own 'crazed brain' is not restored, nor my 'frenzied dreams dispelled' when not even the Irish chronicles of the saints can agree on which Fillan worked where. Out of a total of sixteen recorded saints of that name, probably two, three or possibly four, worked in Scotland—and left traces of their presence. As it is next to impossible to differentiate their spheres of labour, or their biographies, with any accuracy, we shall deal with them all in this note.

We read of an early sixth-century Faolan or Fillan who is named as of 'Ratherann in Scotland and Cill Fhaelain' and whose festival day is 20 June. He it is that Oengus mentions in his *Felire* as 'the splendid mute' and who had the nickname of 'Labar' which could mean either 'the leper' or 'the stammerer'. This name could arise if the missionary was trying to preach or to communicate with a native Briton or Pict while he himself was used to speaking in his native Goidhaelic; but there may, of course, have been

some congenital speech defect. In the note on
Kentigerna the story is recounted of her son
Fillan whose father was so appalled by his
appearance as a baby that he ordered him to be
drowned in case he would develop into a monster. It is suggested there that the story was out of
context for that Fillan, and might it not apply to
this Fillan of Rath Earn? And might not a bad
hare-lip lie behind the story? A further tradition
that he was born with a stone in his mouth
reinforces the feeling that he had some speech
defect.

We need not lay great stress on the claim that
he came of the royal family of Munster as it
became the custom to claim such royal connections for all Celtic saints, but he probably was a
Munsterman and was said to be one of twenty-
two missionaries sent to Scotland by St Ailbe.
About his work we know nothing except his
connections with Loch Earn, and this is con-
firmed by the name of the delightful village at the
end of the loch and by other place-names
mentioned below which suggest the area of his
work.

The second Fillan is of the eighth century and
we know a little more of his life and work. He was
of noble birth, son of Feradach, an Irish prince,
and Kentigerna, daughter of the king of Leinster.
In the note on St Comgan the story is told of how
Fillan accompanied his uncle to Scotland and
assisted in his work in Lochalsh where several
dedications to him are adjacent to others in
memory of St Comgan. He may also be the Fillan
who was patron of the church of Houston in
Renfrewshire, but his main work lay in the glen of
the Dochart and the strath of the Tay. At
Tyndrum the little river is the Fillan Water and
beside Strathfillan church is the saint's well, the

Holy Pool, which Scott names in the verse we quoted. It was for centuries noted for the cure of mental diseases. Nearer Crianlarich are ruins of a mediaeval priory named after the saint and perhaps it was from a cell on this site that he set out on his missionary tours.

The whole length of this valley remembered this saint with affection until long after the Reformation. At Killin, where the church bears his name, his festival was kept as a holiday for the mill workers who believed that he had begun the local market and built the first mill.

One of the most romantic stories of the Celtic saints surrounds Fillan's Five Relics. 'Dewar' which later became a surname was the Gaelic term for the hereditary keeper of a saint's staff, bell, book, or other relic and as these became precious after the saint's death, the 'deor' (or 'dewar') became an important person, and often held land in virtue of his office, which became hereditary. In Fillan's case there were five relics, each with its own custodian living in different parts of the valley. The crozier was known as the 'quigrich' or 'coigreach'—perhaps from the Gaelic for 'stranger' as it was carried by the deor to any place where property or cattle had been stolen and was considered powerful in securing its return. The quigrich lost its staff but the richly ornamented case for the crook survived the Reformation, hidden and forgotten except by the very small number of Catholics remaining in the valleys. At the end of the eighteenth century when Macdonnell led his clansmen out to Upper Canada and helped them to build the township of St Raphael in Glengarry County, Ontario, he took the quigrich with him. He became the first Catholic bishop of Upper Canada and the ancient Scottish relic had a part in some of the solemn ceremonies of ordination. Today one may stand within the ruins of the bishop's basilica in St Raphael township and think of the part the quigrich played in the faith of those emigrants from the Highlands. Later, as archbishop, he took the relic to his new cathedral at Toronto and eventually it was rightly returned to Scotland where it may be seen in the Museum of Antiquities in Edinburgh.

St Fillan's bell, the 'bernane', had the reputation for miraculous cures. After the Reformation it lay uncared for on a tombstone, was carried in 1798 to Hertfordshire, restored to the custody of the Earl of Crawford and eventually joined the staff in the museum. Of the other relics, what exactly the 'meser' and the 'ferg' were is not known; the 'mayne' was the silver shrine, shaped like, and containing, the saint's hand and forearm. The tradition was that while Fillan was alive he could write in his cell in the dark as his arm would shine with a brilliant light. The historian Boece tells of the part this relic played in Bruce's victory at Bannockburn.

The name Fillan occurs in a number of Fife dedications which has led Dr A. B. Scott to postulate a third saint distinct from those with which we have dealt. Pittenweem was an ancient Celtic community where a Fillan was the abbot, and along the coast at Aberdour the parish was his. Today the beautifully-restored church is proud of his name. Forgan was also under his patronage. Others feel that he was one of the Fillans we have mentioned—probably Kentigerna's son who was linked with Fife in an Irish chronicle which mentions Comgan and Fillan together at Glendarshy which, it claims, was in Fife. Another source points to a Glendeochquhy which looks suspiciously like an attempt at Glendochart. We cannot be more definite about this saint, nor can we determine which Fillan left several dedications in Wigtown-shire and the south west. In the note on Comgan it was suggested that it might be his nephew, and they might date from soon after the arrival from Ireland. The distance across the channel is not great and the name Fillan was so common it might almost have been any of the saints of that name who later became so honoured.

In conclusion, here are some of the many Fillan place-names in Scotland.

Almost certainly connected with Fillan of Strath-fillan are Tyndrum, Killin, Struan, Luncarty(?), Glen Fhaolinn and Inverfhaolinn in Glen Etive. Probably also connected with the same saint are Killilan (Kintail), Killinallan (Cille-n'-Fhaelan) (Islay).

Probably connected with Fillan of Loch Earn are St Fillans, Dunfurn, Dunfillan Hill and St Fillan's Choir (Comrie).

Fillan names in Fife, perhaps connected with one of the above, are Aberdour, Pittenweem (Oratory of St Fillan), Forgan (also called St Phillans).

Other Fillan names include Kilallan parish (Ren-frew), Skelmorlie (a chapel), Oxton (Gilfalyn), Sorbie (Wigtownshire) (which has Fillan as patron), Kilfillan (New Luce).

Fillan is found in several places in Galloway as a farm name.

The festival date for Fillan of Loch Earn is 22 June, while Fillan of Strathfillan has 9 or 19 January.

A. P. Forbes, *Kalendars of Scottish Saints*, 1872

G. A. F. Knight, *Archaeological Light on the Early Christianising of Scotland*, 1933

A. B. Scott, *The Pictish Nation*, 1918

Finian

Adamnan and other early writers use the nickname Finbar for this saint, which means 'bald-pate', and other variants of the name are Barr, Winning and Wynnian. Although the Celtic Church had several missionaries named Finian, the biography we shall outline here is that of the sixth-century St Finian of Magh Bile (Moville) near Newtownards in County Down.

Finian came of Ulster stock, perhaps from the slopes of the Slieve Croob hills, for as a boy he attracted the interest of the famous Colman of Dromore, who took him along to Strangford Lough to the monastic school on the island of Nendrum to be educated under its abbot St Caolan. The site of this school, famous till its destruction by the Vikings, has been excavated and pens, slates and other equipment are displayed in Belfast museum, tangible remains from young Finian's schooldays. In line with the strict discipline of Celtic monasteries and schools, Finian was on one occasion 'touching toes' ready to experience Caolan's rod when the master, to his surprise, found his arm remained locked in mid air, still holding the cane. 'Why do you not do what you set out to do and cane me?' the old manuscript makes young Finian ask, as he looked up at the teacher. 'I would, holy boy, but the Holy Ghost is restraining me,' replied the saint, apparently dismissing the possibility of it being an acute and sudden rheumatic attack caused by a damp, unheated monastery. Caolan had no alternative but to remit the punishment, and the responsibility of continuing to educate such a remarkable boy was so daunting that noting that 'at that very moment certain ships were approaching from the "Magnum Monasterium" (Candida Casa)', he sent Finian off with them to complete his education at that more famous seminary under Nennio and later under Mugint.

It was probably during his last years at the school at Candida Casa (Whithorn) that he received a severe rebuke from Mugint for his part in a rather unsavoury incident in connection with a girl scholar (some Celtic schools were always coeducational), Drusticc, daughter of a Pictish chief. There are several versions in the old manuscripts but the most likely is that she was much in love with Finian and almost blackmailed him into going to her room to sleep with her. He, however, was not interested and sent one of his friends; when the girl was found to be pregnant the storm broke and all in the plot, including Finian, incurred Mugint's wrath.

It is said that Finian was so renowned for his learning that he remained as tutor at Candida Casa for twenty years, travelling widely through Scotland and founding many 'muinntirs'. About 540 he went back to Strangford and founded the monastery of Magh Bile (Moville) at the head of the lough, a few miles from Nendrum where he had received his first schooling.

To Moville in later days came a young novice from Derry—Columcille or Columba, so giving a continuous educational link from Ninian to the founder of Iona. If there be any truth in the story of Columba copying a psalm from Finian's new Jerome psalter it almost certainly happened here.

The many Scottish place-names commemorating Finian may be due, writes P. A. Wilson, to confusion with an Ayrshire missionary, Winnin, or they may arise from a later cultus or from places he visited during his period at Whithorn.

By the rocky shores of Luce Bay in the parish of Mochrum, near Whithorn, and across the water from Magh Bile stand the foundations and walls of a very ancient chapel, Chipperfinnian. Not far off, in Girthon parish, is Loch Whinyon while in Stewartry is the parish called Kirkgunzeon (the 'z' is silent or sounded like old Scots 'y') and nearby is Kylliemingan, both variants of Finian, as may be the hotel at Powmill (Kinross) called Gartwhinzean. In northern districts, for some reason, the name appears in forms like Fymbar or St Bar. In Ayrshire, Kilwinning has Finian on the arms of the former burgh and there is Lochwinnoch. On Bute is a Kilwhinleck.

Finian's festival is 10 September.

G. A. F. Knight, *Archaeological Light on the Early Christianising of Scotland*, 1933

H. C. Lawlor, *The Monastery of St Mochaoi*, 1925

D. Pochin Mould, *The Irish Saints*, 1964

ſinᴛan munnu was a younger contemporary and cousin of the great Columcille and a descendant of Niall of the Nine Hostages. He was a leper, although exactly what form of skin disease is meant by this term is not now clear, and certainly it did not appear to hinder his missionary work or compel his isolation. After training under some of the great Celtic teachers he decided to join Columba on Iona. Unfortunately, when he arrived he found Columba had died and his successor Baithene refused to accept Fintan as he said Columba had warned him that the new recruit should be no monk but a full abbot. Fintan then returned to Ireland and founded the great monastery of Teachmunnu (the house of Munnu). Behind this story may possibly lie the thought that Fintan might have been Columba's successor as head of the Iona monasteries but for health or other reasons he made way for Baithene.

In a sinister folk-lore tale, it is said that Columba ordered Fintan's father to cast the child from a cliff into the sea. He obeys, but Kenneth, arriving just in time, rescues the baby and denounces Columba for cruelty. Later, Columba foretells a great and saintly future for the child and as Kenneth is dying it is Fintan who gives him the viaticum. For centuries Fintan Munnu's 'baculus' was preserved beside the church on the Holy Loch bearing his name. Around Loch Fyne we find several Kilmuns which indicate, if not the saint's actual presence, at least that his cult was active in the district.

In one of the most romantic and beautiful parts of the Highlands where Loch Leven narrows at Ballachulish is the ancient chapel of St Mund on the island of Eilean Munde, and the *Felire of Oengus* pays tribute to him:

> Fintan–the torch with the ascending flame, pure tested gold . . . a warrior, religious and tortured with pain.

In the controversy about the date of Easter he was for the ancient Celtic usage, opposing the revised Roman dating.

Fintan Munnu's festival is 21 October.

D. H. Farmer, *Oxford Dictionary of Saints,* 1978

A. P. Forbes, *Kalendars of Scottish Saints,* 1872

G. A. F. Knight, *Archaeological Light on the Early Christianising of Scotland,* 1933

George St George of England suffered martyrdom, probably in the third or fourth century, at Lydda in Palestine. The popular and widely known incident of his slaying a dragon has almost resulted in the dragon slaying the saint, for it is now recognised as a variant of a common folk-myth, which has persuaded some scholars to regard George himself as merely legendary without historical reality. The fact, however, that the saint was a popular figure among Eastern Christians for six hundred years before the dragon appeared about the twelfth century suggests that he was a real figure, but all details of his life-story soon faded and were replaced by the dragon incident which appears in widely differing versions. The problem of who St George was is further complicated by confusion with a heretical George of Cappadocia of the same period who was murdered by the orthodox Christians of Alexandria.

The story tells how a certain king, either of Libya or Syria, found that his people were being plagued by a fierce, wild dragon. In an effort to appease this dragon the farm stock were over a period all fed to him, followed by the local children. It then came to the turn of the king's own maiden daughter. She set out bravely to offer herself to the monster, but before she could reach the den a knight in shining armour appeared and offered to engage the monster in combat. As might be expected the saint was the

winner and returned to town leading the defeated
beast by a rope with the princess safely by his
side.

This legend is said by scholars to have its
origin in the Greek myth of Perseus and
Andromeda (retold by Charles Kingsley in *The
Heroes*), and a Celtic variant is the tale of the
farmer's daughters of Pitempton, near Dundee,
who were rescued by another Christian knight,
Martin.

St George's popularity increased greatly from
the time of the Crusades, when Richard
Lionheart of England, to whom St George
appeared in a vision, restored the church at
Lydda wherein his bones rested but which had
been destroyed by the Saracens. The same vision
appeared at the siege of Jerusalem:

> then come St George, clothyd yn whyte and a red cross on
> his brest and yode up the laddyrs and bade the cristen
> men com affyr hym.

The collar of the Order of The Garter, founded
by Edward III, portrays George with the defeated
dragon and gradually he became accepted as
patron saint of England. Edward I, in his invasion
of Scotland, had his supporting ships fly the St
George's ensign, the red cross on white which is
the flag of the city of London. In 1606 James VI
and I placated rivalry between his sailors by
commanding them to fly on the mainmasts the
St George and St Andrew crosses interlaced,
each flying their own flag at the stern.

The first mention of George from Scotland is in
the little-known book *Concerning the Holy
Places,* written by St Adamnan who had himself
never been to the East but who got material from
Arculf, a Gaulish bishop. It mentions a knight
who 'commended himself and his horse to St
George' but veneration of the saint made little

progress in Scotland probably because he had been adopted by her English rivals.

The mediaeval church of Dundee had a chantry to the saint founded by David Lindsay, first Earl of Crawford and there were altars or chantries at Brechin, St Nicholas (Aberdeen) and Dunkeld, where Bishop George Brown in 1510 built in his honour a hospital for seven old men and a chapel and school, donating also a bell bearing his name. For a period George was patron of the church at Abernethy on Spey.

Nine churches in the *Church of Scotland Year Book* are dedicated to the saint but none is of historic note. Hawick, Dumfries, Paisley, Greenock, Montrose and Aberdeen, each has its St George's. Edinburgh had as part of its New Town legacy the massive St George's in Charlotte Square, which so effectively closed off George Street at the west end. It is now part of the Scottish Record Office. The name is continued in St Andrew's and St George's further along the street. Glasgow has St George's Tron and St George's-in-the-Fields. The former was notable by its prominent site in Buchanan Street and its four strange obelisks which Stark, the architect, had intended to replace by statues of the evangelists. It was also noted for the ministry of the evangelist Tom Allen till his early death.

Streets and churches in the New Town of Edinburgh were named at random from members of the royal family or from saints so it is not now possible to tell if the king or the saint was intended when George Street was named. The Episcopal St George's Chapel, erected before the parish church on the south side of York Place, was a remarkable round building, but about half a century ago it was sold and disguised with a more normal frontage. Its people then merged into the larger Episcopal building on the north side of the street.

St George's festival is 23 April.

D. H. Farmer, *Oxford Dictionary of Saints*, 1978

Gerardine

Reputed to be of the race of Cruithni—the so-called Irish Picts—Gerardine is said to have fled before the Danes and Norsemen and sought refuge at Kinnedor in Moray. Legend claimed that in the building of his simple cell the saint was helped by a flood which floated the timber down to the exact spot where it could be of use.

On the coast near Lossiemouth may be seen the headland which became known as Holyman's Head from his presence there, and the adjacent cave is St Gerardine's cave. It is said that a chapel in the cave was destroyed over a century ago by a drunken sailor. Lossiemouth considered itself under Gerardine's protection and incorporated in its arms the figure of the saint patrolling the beach on a night of storm watching for signs of any wreck to which he might offer assistance.

Miraculous events from the common stock of the mediaeval hagiographer have been introduced to fill the many gaps in the saint's biography. One such story tells that while Gerardine was ploughing, a wolf stole up and ate one of the pair of oxen, whereupon it was ordered by Gerardine to take the ox's place in the harness—a miracle which is repeated in the story of Ninian.

The date of the saint's death is said to be 934. The festival is 8 November.

D. H. Farmer, *Oxford Dictionary of Saints*, 1978

ꝺERMⱯNUS

Almost certainly the most learned, and probably the most able, of all the figures whom we have included as 'saints' in this volume is St Germain or Germanus. He was already an advocate and doctor of Roman law before turning to the Church. Born about 378 he was appointed bishop of the see of Auxerre (Auxiliodunum) in Gaul in 418.

About the beginning of the fifth century the western Church had become greatly troubled by the rapid spread of the Pelagian heresy, and Germanus, whose orthodoxy and scholarship were both above suspicion, was sent to Britain to restore Catholicism. Pelagius himself was a Briton and the heresy which took firm root in these islands centred on the sinful nature of man and the necessity for the grace of Christ in man's salvation. It is difficult for us today to imagine the strength of feeling aroused by what seems to us merely an academic theological point. But if we look below the surface we shall find it is still important enough to divide Churches and the folk in them. Pelagius could not accept that man's nature was altogether evil and felt that within him were aspects both of evil and of good. This doctrine at first seems harmless enough but theologians were quick to point out that once it is accepted that men could by their own efforts rise above sin in life, Christ's offer of forgiveness and full salvation becomes only an 'optional extra' in religion. Grace becomes a triviality.

The argument, of course, advanced far beyond this simplification. The argument against Pelagius stressed that Grace was at the heart of the Christian faith; against this Pelagians pointed out that man must never remain without straining every effort to put sin away from him. Like many theological battles, truth lies some way between the extremes.

Constantius of Lyons, who wrote a *Life* of Germanus, is tantalising in the lack of geographical detail about where in Britain the bishop went searching for heretics. He mentions a visit to the shrine of the first martyr, Alban, which made scholars look for his tracks in the east country, but scholars are now looking more to Wales and the west. There he is remembered in many places under the name Garmon or Harmon. A very ancient tradition in connection with Patrick suggested that Germanus either ordained or consecrated the patron of Ireland or was present at the occasion. To get Patrick and Germanus together most of the early biographies of Patrick take him over to Gaul. We know, however, that Germanus was in Britain in 429, a very likely date for such a meeting. In the Journal *Folklore* (1979, Pt I), I have suggested a remote spot in the Berwyn Mountains as a possibility. Llanharmon Dyfferin Cieriog has an ancient church within a Celtic-type rath and its Germanus place-name is very old. There are so many Garmon and Harmon place-names in north Wales and Man that some scholars have suggested that they derive not from Germanus but from an otherwise unknown St Germon.

It is possible that either during Germanus' visit in 429 or a later visit about 447 he visited Scotland, as the heresy was strong there. If he did we have only one place-name to remind us of it. As the trains on the east-coast route approach Edinburgh's Waverley station, a glimpse may be had of St Germains signal box and level crossing, named after the neighbouring estate.

After the saint's death his cult spread widely, bringing a multiplicity of place-names which had no connection with Germanus on his British visits.

His festival is 31 July.

D. H. Farmer, *Oxford Dictionary of Saints*, 1978
E. S. Towill, 'Isle of Youth and the Baculus Iesu of Patrick' in *Folklore*, Part I, 1979

giles Visitors to Edinburgh express surprise that the metropolitan church of the capital, the great city of Scottish Presbyterianism, bears the name not of Scotland's patron, St Andrew, nor of her Celtic missioner, Columba, but of an obscure French Benedictine monk.

The cult of St Giles (Egidius or Aegidius in Latin) was brought to Britain during the period of the Crusades. From 1096 the preaching of Peter the Hermit, with the great rallying call 'Deus vult' (God wills it), brought thousands of men to Palestine from the European countries to regain the Holy Land for Christ from the Saracens. For almost two centuries there were constant contingents of Scots—crusaders, pilgrims, traders and camp-followers—travelling through France to embark at the Mediterranean ports. Their route was down the Rhone valley to Arles near which the abbey town of St Gilles, on a bend in the river, was rapidly becoming the main port of embarkation.

The saint whose shrine made the great abbey a place of pilgrimage was a somewhat shadowy figure from four centuries earlier. Born at Athens it was said that Giles had built a primitive grotto near Arles but fled to Spain to escape the crowds which gathered when they recognised him as a saint and miracle worker. Later he returned to the district, living as a hermit at a remote spot up the Rhone with only a hind as companion. Once, when the king, Flavius Wanda, was hunting, he aimed at the hind but the arrow pierced the arm of Giles who was close by, trying to protect the frightened animal.

Wanda gave Giles land in the valley, which in the king's honour was thereafter called the Valley Flavian, and a Benedictine monastery was built, with Giles as leader of the community. About this time (around 673) the area was devastated by the Musselman invasions of south Europe and the monastery was destroyed. Giles fled with the sacred vessels to Orleans, where he came under the protection of the powerful emperor, Charles Martel, who helped him to return to Arles and rebuild on a grander scale the little church and monastery. Here Giles died about the year 725. The place, which had both Greek and Roman associations, had been named Heraclée but soon became known as Saint Gilles.

Many miraculous stories were told of Giles, and his cult grew in popularity. Prayer to him was supposed to be particularly efficacious in curing children of fear of the dark, and he was remembered as a simple, gracious and pious figure. His symbol was the arrow and he was often accompanied by his hind, which appears as a bearer in the arms of the former city of Edinburgh.

Probably many crusaders prayed in the great church of St Gilles for safety on their journey. On their return to Scotland they would remember him and request further favours from him. In England no less than 146 churches were dedicated to him, outstanding among which was St Giles, Cripplegate, near London Wall. The area was badly blitzed during the war but the church has been beautifully restored, with the statue of the saint over the porch.

In Edinburgh, during the reign of Alexander I, a new church was erected for the citizens and it was probably then that the patronage of the French saint began. The queen, Sibylla, was the daughter of the English king Henry, whose queen, Matilda, had introduced Giles to London and built a leper hospital bearing his name. It would be natural for the Scots queen to emulate her English mother-in-law, but there is no certain link to prove that this happened. Giles was popular among the Benedictines and there were other dedications to him in Scotland, including Elgin, where the massive Georgian church still bears his name.

The likeness of the saint in St Giles, Edinburgh, is said to have been life-size and of outstanding workmanship. In the fifteenth century, William Preston of Gourton brought an arm bone of the saint from France and presented it to the town. Annually, on the saint's day, the great image and the arm bone in its shrine were carried round in procession. Concerning this, David Lindsay wrote:

> Fy on you fostereris of idolatrie,
> That til ane deid stik does sik reverence
> In presens of the pepill publicklie.

But five years after he had written this, in 1558, riot broke out during the procession. The statue was first ducked in the Nor Loch and then burned, and soon after the silverwork, jewels and vestments were stripped from the image and the arm, and were sold for the repair of the church. There were to be no more records in the town accounts such as there had been previously:

> for paynting of Sanct Gell . . . for mending and polishing Sanct Gell's arm.

The official title of the church everybody calls St Giles' cathedral is the High Kirk of Edinburgh and this is always used in the Church Courts. It was only a cathedral, in the sense of being the seat of a bishop, for a few years when Charles I created Edinburgh an episcopal see. Under Presbyterianism the term 'cathedral' is no more than honorary, as each minister enjoys the full status and responsibilities of the ministry and there are no diocesan bishops. The Roman Catholic and the Scottish Episcopal Churches both have cathedrals in Edinburgh, both St Mary's.

St Giles, Elgin, is an older foundation than Elgin cathedral. Its heavy stone vaulting collapsed in 1679 on the day of the battle of Bothwell Bridge. Ormiston and Dundonald parishes both claim St Giles and there were several chapels.

His festival is 1 September.

D. Attwater, *Penguin Dictionary of Saints*, 1965

F. L. Cross and E. A. Livingstone (eds), *Oxford Dictionary of the Christian Church*, 1974

ᵹodric, known as the hermit of Finchale,

was not born a hermit nor did he show signs of becoming one in boyhood or even in early manhood. He tasted many of the pleasures of the world before he found his peace with man and with God—which is probably the ideal way to pass through life. Of Godric an unkind critic commented, 'as dirty an old man as ever became a saint', but this is far from the truth. Even when, after middle life, he found a quiet corner of the woods by the River Wear at Finchale and built his 'desertum', he erected a bath, but screened it for privacy from the wild things.

This remarkably interesting man was born in the Midlands of England and for some years was a pedlar and chapman, wandering up into the Scottish Borders and having such success with his sales that he became a capitalist in a modest way. At this period of life he loved travel and made pilgrimages to the continent and the Holy Land. Learning also attracted him and we hear that, for a time, he attached himself to the choir school at Durham. As a sideline he seems to have owned some boats until, in the light of a developing conscience, he re-examined all his previous methods (which may have been rather shady), sold up his business and almost literally burnt his boats. When in old age the good monk Reginald of Durham told the hermit he was about to write his life, Godric half humorously offered to supply headings for the chapters:

> Godric is a country clod and fat. He used to be a fornicator, adulterer and a dirty hound who practised usury in his business dealings and gave false measure and deceived the unwary. Now he is a hermit, but a hypocrite, a solitary whose head is crowded with vile thoughts, a glutton and covetous fellow . . . Godric likes his ease and can be found both day and night snoring luxuriously . . . Write these and worse things about Godric if you would show him to the world for the monster he is.

All this, of course, is a very exaggerated picture of the subject of Reginald's great biography. We are also given a picture of the physical appearance of the Hermit of Finchale:

> He had a broad forehead, sparkling grey eyes, bushy eyebrows which almost met. Oval face, long nose and bushy beard. He was always slow to speak, eager to listen and sympathetic to those in trouble.

Godric knew the countryside of southern Scotland well, his favourite town was St Andrews and not only did he visit it and other towns when he carried a pack but he later liked sailing the coast. For a time he lived wild in the dense forests round Carlisle and the Debatable Lands and was nearly beaten to death by Scots troopers. Once he fell into the River Wear and nearly drowned.

Devotion to St Cuthbert particularly attracted him and on his way to St Andrews he would stop and spend time in prayer on Cuthbert's island of Farne.

When Godric's fame spread, many notables found their way to think and talk with the remarkable and very human hermit. For the last years of his life he built a quiet retreat at a bend of the River Wear. Here he kept many wild creatures who recognised in him a friend. Almost alone among humans he loved reptiles and the place became known for these creeping creatures who befriended the saint. He always loved the Benedictine Rule and after his day the Benedictines built the great priory at Finchale where his desertum had been.

He died at Finchale in 1170 on 21 May, which is taken as his festival.

J. Broderick, *A Procession of Saints*, 1947
D. H. Farmer, *Oxford Dictionary of Saints*, 1978

ꝪORᴅIAN At the head of the long and

beautiful valley of the Manor Water in Peeblesshire there stood, until the eighteenth century, a seemly little parish kirk dedicated to an obscure Roman saint and martyr of the second or third century. This was the lad Gordianus or Gorgham whose name appeared as a martyr alongside St Epimachus but about whom nothing seemed to be known. It was said they were victims of the apostate Emperor Julian. The surviving acts of these saints, Forbes suggests, are legendary and worthless. He even suggests the dedication of the church in Manor Valley might have been to a different figure, the eunuch of the palace, Gorgon.

The old church survived till the eighteenth century when no other than Walter Scott's father was instrumental in having it demolished to provide road material. A few furnishings, it was said, were removed to the new church down the valley.

Gordian's festival is 10 May.

A. P. Forbes, *Kalendars of Scottish Saints*, 1872
A. and J. Lang, *Highways and Byways in the Borders*, 1923

hERbERT Perhaps (like his close friend, St Cuthbert) originally from the monastery of Old Maelros, little is known about Herbert except that he and Cuthbert were wont to meet annually for prayer and meditation. It is likely that Cuthbert acted to him as 'anamchara' or soul-friend. In 686 they met in Carlisle where Cuthbert had gone to console the queen after the slaying of her husband Egfrid at the battle of Dunnichen or Nechtansmere near Forfar. Herbert is also known as the Hermit of Derwentwater.

Cuthbert and Herbert had prayed that as they had been friends in life so in death they might not be separated, and indeed, in 687 they both passed away on the same day, Herbert on his lonely little island in the Lake District, the more famous Cuthbert away on the Farnes.

B. Colgrave and R. A. B. Mynors (eds), *Bede: Historia Ecclesiastica*, 1969
H. Mayr-Harting, *The Coming of Christianity*, 1972

hilda was the most eminent among the remarkable circle of talented, Anglo-Saxon women who graced the Northumbrian churches during the seventh century. Born in 614, she was related by blood to the Northumbrian and East Anglian royal families. She was baptised by Paulinus but was slow to enter the monastic life.

However, she made up for this by devoting the second half of her working years to playing a most prominent part in the monasteries, first as abbess of Hartlepool, then, after 657, at Whitby. Under Hilda this double or 'coeducational' foundation became famous for the bishops it produced and the scholarship it encouraged. In 663–4, under her lead, it acted as host to the important synod which decided between the Celtic or Roman Church usages. Although Hilda was in favour of the former she accepted the final decision which was for Rome.

She encouraged the poet Caedmon and led the female, high-born religious leaders among whom were Abba, Bega and others; questions about the ordination of women seemingly did not arise.

Hilda died in 680, and her cult remained strong in the north of England, with no less than fifteen parishes under her patronage. Whitby (Streanaeshalch) was sacked by the Danes about 800 but arose as an abbey in the eleventh century. Hilda's relics were claimed by both Glastonbury and Gloucester.

Hilda's festival day is 17 November.

H. Mayr-Harting, *The Coming of Christianity*, 1972

John the baptist

The name of St John is commemorated in many of our parishes and churches, both ancient and modern, but often it is by no means clear whether the Baptist or the Evangelist is intended. In older churches a clue may be found if the festival date is known. Any church where 24 June or 29 August is significant in its history refers to St John the Baptist. By early tradition Midsummer Day was set apart as his festival, as he was supposed to have prophesied of Christ, 'It is right the he should grow greater while I grow less', and this was seen symbolically in the shortening of the autumn days. The usual festival date for a saint, however, was his death day—his birth into fuller life—and as John was said to have suffered martyrdom on 29 August that day was held in his memory in certain places.

John, the last of the Prophets and the first to point out the Lamb of God, is our link between Old Testament Judaism and the Christian Church. The gospel records of his life, and especially of his baptism of Jesus in the Jordan, have taken on new interest since 1947, when a Bedouin herd boy discovered a number of large jars containing scrolls with ancient Hebrew writing in a cave at Qum'Ran by the Dead Sea. Not only were other caves and more manuscripts found but nearby the foundations of a monastery dating from the time of Christ were excavated. This proved to be the headquarters of an ascetic Jewish sect of which probably John himself was

113

a member. Baptismal tanks and fragments of leather girdles were among the discoveries and the site, north of the Dead Sea, corresponded to the traditional place of Jesus' baptism in the Jordan.

Mark's gospel (chapter 6) gives a detailed account of John's arrest and execution, probably in the grim fortress of Machaerus. The account suggests that for a time John's disciples maintained a separate community from those of Jesus, with whom it is possible they later merged. Today a small sect in south Iraq, numbering only a few thousand, known as Mandaeans or Christians of St John, hold the Baptist in high honour and claim descent from these followers.

Although John's death did not result from any confession of faith in Christ but from his fearless proclamation of moral values, he is usually classed among the Christian martyrs. In art he is portrayed pointing to a lamb—the Agnus Dei (John 1: 35).

Later his festival at midsummer incorporated many customs originally pagan. In the parish of Urquhart blazing torches used to be carried through the fields to secure a good harvest, and sprays of St John's wort were gathered the previous evening and brought into the houses as protection against evil. In the year 1314 the battle of Bannockburn was fought on our saint's festival and before it King Robert the Bruce prayed assistance from the Baptist and St Andrew.

Perth has always had links with John the Baptist and was referred to often as St Johnstoun. Its parish church was correctly known as the Kirk of the Holy Cross of St John the Baptist because of its cross-shaped building. This pre-Reformation church, worthily restored, was once the scene of Knox's famous sermon against idolatry, which, in spite of his calls for moderation, led to much iconoclasm. The town seal depicted John in a camel-hair tunic holding the Agnus Dei.

The village of Dalry in the Stewartry of Kirkcudbright is correctly St John's Town (or St John's Clachan) of Dalry. In 1547 James IV gave an offering to the priest of St John's Kirk at Dalry which he passed on pilgrimage to St Ninian's shrine at Whithorn.

Corstorphine parish church incorporates an ancient chapel of St John the Baptist built by Sir Adam Forrester before 1405. Enlarged by his son, the chapel became a collegiate church. The parish church near the chapel had become ruinous by the year 1646 and the chapel was rebuilt to form the present church. In 1828 the building was ruthlessly 'improved' by the Edinburgh architect William Burn but restored again more thoughtfully at the beginning of this century, with the ancient chapel as the chancel.

The Hospitallers, or Knights, of St John of Jerusalem (introduced to Scotland by David I) still hold the preceptory of Torphichen as their principal house. Today their functions are largely charitable but in their early days the knights wielded considerable power. They also had a chapel dedicated to St John at Inverness and another at Drem. In Edinburgh Sir John Crawford erected a chapel to the saint on the Boroughmuir which became incorporated in the Convent of St Katherine in the Sciennes. A district of the Pleasance, now rebuilt, was known as St John's Hill.

F. L. Cross and E. A. Livingstone, *Oxford Dictionary of the Christian Church*, 1974

J. Grant, *Old and New Edinburgh*, 1883

john the evangelist

Of whom are we thinking when we speak of St John the Evangelist? The New Testament contains five documents traditionally associated with the name of John—the fourth gospel, three short letters and the book called Revelation of St John the Divine or the Apocalypse. Of these, neither the gospel nor the first letter reveals their author; the other two short letters indicate that their writer was John the Elder; while the Apocalypse simply states that it was a vision of 'John'. The tradition that all these writings were from the pen of the fisherman-apostle, the son of Zebedee, is difficult to accept and there is no particular religious virtue in feeling that it has to be accepted.

The language and thought of the Book of Revelation is very different from that of the gospel and the letters, which have much the same style of Greek and reflect the same religious thought. The Greek, and the thought, of Revelation is rapid, pungent, excitable and reflects the distress of a period of persecution. It seems unlikely that all were written by the same author.

The great fourth gospel is a document of deep philosophic thought, drawing upon both Greek and Jewish learning and devotion; its author evidently knew Jerusalem and district well and might himself have been a member of the Jewish Sanhedrin or Supreme Court. He seems to veil his identity by referring to himself as the 'disciple whom Jesus cared about'. Is it not likely that he was one of the group of Jerusalem disciples which included Joseph of Arimathea, Nicodemus and others? The writer seems to end his work at the conclusion of chapter 20 and the last chapter, by an editor, refers to him as 'the witness'. The writer of Revelation speaks of himself as working as a slave in the Roman mines on Patmos and he addresses the Churches at Ephesus and Asia Minor with authority. There is some evidence that about the end of the first century there were two disciples of the name of John in Ephesus and both gospel (with the letters) and Revelation seem to have originated in this area.

In the early Church, its western element (centred on Rome) began to look on St Peter as its leader and inspirer while the Churches in the east, Antioch and Alexandria, tended to look to St John. The western Church prided itself on orthodoxy, methodical thinking, uniformity and what we might call a businesslike approach in its thought and worship. The eastern Churches, which believed John to be their exemplar, placed less stress on organisation, were more diversified in thought and worship and were anxious to be seen to put more stress on the spirit rather than the letter of the law in the Church.

From its earliest days the Scottish Church has tended towards the eastern rather than the western interpretation of the faith, which may in part be due to its contacts with Gaulish Christianity which had drawn much from the east. Parts of the liturgy and details of dress and ritual showed eastern influence in the period commonly known as the Celtic until it was brought into uniformity with the rest of Europe after the synod of Whitby. Even after that event, for some centuries the Scottish Church tended to look to St John rather than St Peter. The great High Cross of Iona, irreparably damaged some years ago, was St John's and for centuries had stood alongside the Cross of St Martin, a saint also under eastern influence. It has often been suggested that John rather than Andrew should have been patron of Scotland.

The Celtic Church early made use of the beasts from the Old Testament Book of Ezekiel and the New Testament Book of Revelation as symbols of the Four Evangelists. John was given the badge of the eagle as showing Christ soaring above the earthly nations—Revelation 8: 13: 'I looked and I heard an eagle crying'. The symbol appears beautifully carved on the ancient oak of St Cuthbert's coffin in Durham cathedral and on the vellum of the books of Kells and Durrow. An alternative symbol for John the Evangelist is a chalice with a viper emerging, illustrating the poisoned wine. Legend told how the saint had drunk from a poisoned cup and remained unharmed. A modern example of the symbolism is in a stained glass window in the former St John's United Free Church, Dundee (now one of the university halls), where the poison escaping from the chalice is seen as a flame.

In the Highlands, commemorations to the Evangelist are often in the Gaelic form—Killean is found at Cheyne, Sutherland, at Loch Spelve (Mull) and at Kintyre. Kildalton, Islay, with a fine High Cross comes from Dulta Moire, the foster-son of Mary, and refers to Christ's charge to the apostle to care for the Virgin. In Shetland, John is remembered at Kirkabister, Gutches, Baleasta and Unst. In Banffshire is St John's Well and his Ford near Chapelton. In Aberdeenshire are a well at Fyvie and a chapel at Tarves. Marykirk has his spring. There is a well at Spott, and chapels at Dunbar and Scotscraig. In Wigtownshire, there are chapels at Old Luce and Inch. Montrose, Kettle and Thankerton all held him as patron.

The above is only a selection of former dedications to St John. The festival on 27 December is so near Christmas that it receives little recognition.

F. L. Cross and E. A. Livingstone (eds), *Oxford Dictionary of the Christian Church*, 1974

J. M. Mackinlay, *Ancient Church Dedications in Scotland*, 1910

Katherine of Alexandria

At the beginning of the fourth century, while his legionaries were still patrolling Hadrian's Wall to keep the Picts from his empire, the Emperor Maxentius put into operation the laws against Christians in the north-African city of Alexandria by imprisoning a maiden, Katherine—putting her 'ynto prison, forto abide ther xxxte dayes wythout meat or drynke' writes an old chronicler. As the girl did not repent nor give up her faith she was condemned to be tied to a revolving wheel set with knives which would tear her to pieces. The legend, which is historically doubtful, goes on to relate that the machine broke down at the critical moment and so Katherine was allowed the more merciful death of beheading. The body was later carried to Mount Sinai where a small monastery was later erected by the great Emperor Justinian.

This, of course, is the origin of the revolving firework still called the Catherine Wheel and in most representations Katherine is shown beside a wheel. Among the mediaeval wall paintings in the church of Foulis-Easter near Dundee, we can still see the saint with a wheel, a sword and a knife.

In spite of the fact that so little was known about her, Katherine became one of the most popular female saints in the mediaeval church and Scotland has many dedications. Two of the most remarkable and most interesting are to be found just south of Edinburgh—St Katherine-in-the-Hopes, and St Katherine-of-the-Kaims. Pentland walkers coming over from Balerno or Colinton pause by the finger-post at the bend at Glencorse reservoir where the path from Logan-lea joins them. Some proceed towards Flotter-stone, but others pause to gaze for a while into the depths of the water, for below, submerged when the valley was dammed, still stand the remains of a chapel, St Katherine-in-the-Hopes. It is rumoured that they may still be seen when the water is very low but few know anyone who has seen them except in imagined reflections if the day be calm.

Tradition asserts that William St Clair of Roslin, in the time of Bruce erected the chapel as a thank-offering to the saint for helping his hounds to catch a white deer before it got across the March Burn. Apparently he was to lose his head if the animal escaped but to gain a great tract of the Pentlands if it turned back. When the deer got halfway over, St Clair, in despair, fell on his knees in prayer to St Katherine; a hound suddenly appeared and headed the animal back and, so the story goes, St Clair became the owner of Logan, Kirkton and Earnscraig.

Despite what animal lovers may think of the story the chapel was erected and served the parish of Glencorse till 1647 when the predeces-sor of the present 'old church' was erected downstream at Earnscraig, the spot so loved by R. L. Stevenson. The building up at the Hopes remained in ruins until submerged in the 1820s when the reservoir was built.

Katherine-of-the-Kaims is now well within the extended boundaries of the city, although it is not many years since the Kaims, now a busy junc-tion, was little more than a smithy and a short row of cottages. Behind this was the estate of St Katherine's with, beyond it, Gracemount farm, all of which is now built up. St Katherine's had a famous balm well which was dedicated to St Margaret. The legend is confused and appears in two main versions. The historian Hector Boece first tells it.

Margaret, Queen of Scotland, had heard of the martyr-saint Katherine and desired that a drop of oil might be brought to her from the monastery of Mount Sinai which was noted for its springs of healing oil. Unfortunately the angel carrying the oil spilled it as she was passing the Kaims, a well of water spouted forth at the spot and Margaret built a little chapel over the well. The water was always covered with a film of oil and pilgrims believed it had curative powers. One of the few places James VI visited when revisiting Scotland after 1603 was the balm well. In 1617 he ordered it to be fenced with stones and a stair built to make approach easier.

The version of the story given in Grant's *Old and New Edinburgh* is even more extraordinary. In it Katherine was apparently a Scottish lady, contemporary with Queen Margaret, who sent her to Mount Sinai with a commission to bring some of the miraculous oil to her. At the Kaims she dropped a little and the well sprang forth. Margaret erected the chapel and Katherine, the lady who had brought the oil, was now also considered to be a saint and was buried beside the spot. There is, however, no sign of any burial and none of the several St Katherine's would fit this version of the story.

Abernethy on Spey absorbed a parish dedicated to Katherine. Both Fortingall and Coupar-Angus abbeys may originally have been dedicated to her. Chapels and altars to Katherine all over Scotland are too numerous to list. The strangely named well in Kirkmaiden (Wigtownshire)—Kibbertie Kite—was thought by Sir Herbert Maxwell to be from Gaelic Tobar Tigh Cait.

There had long been doubts about the historicity of the African Katherine and in 1969 her cultus was suppressed. In legend Katherine was noted for her wisdom, was reputed to have defeated fifty sages in debate and was therefore considered patron of all philosophers (as well, of course, as wheel-wrights). It was said she so impressed the Emperor Maxentius by her learning that he proposed marriage—as an alternative he had her beheaded.

D. H. Farmer, *Oxford Dictionary of Saints*, 1978
C. Williams, *Saints: Their Cults and Origins*, 1980

katherine of siena

A much later Katherine than Katherine of Alexandria was also remembered in Edinburgh. The district in the south side called the Sciennes (pronounced 'sheens') once possessed the Dominican convent of nuns of St Katherine of Siena. This saint, who became noted both for public activities and for personal mystical devotion, was born at Siena in Italy about 1347. She joined the 'Black Nuns' and later played a prominent part in supporting Pope Urban VI in the 'great schism' when two rivals fought for the papel throne. The writings which survive show Katherine to have been outstanding in intellect and remarkable in her ability to combine deep personal piety with political activity.

Sciennes is an understandable corruption of Siena. Marmion, looking down from Blackford Hill, calls the convent 'St Katherine's of Scienne', while Sir David Lindsay, finding no corruption in their house, makes Chastity flee for refuge to 'the Sisteris of the Schenis'. Founded in 1517 by Lady Seton, whose husband had been killed at Flodden, the buildings stood on the south of the Boroughloch, approximately on the site of St Catherine's Place. The first prioress of the convent was Josina Henryson. She maintained strict discipline and no breath of scandal was ever raised against the community. At the gateway from Causewayside stood a small chapel of St John the Baptist which had been erected only five years earlier by Sir John Crawford who himself officiated in the chapel and acted as chaplain to the nuns. The donation deed stipulated that the chaplain should always be of his name or family and should wear a white cassock with a portraiture of the Baptist.

In 1544 the convent suffered in the English attack on the town, and after being rebuilt, enjoyed only just over twenty years of active life until the reformers drove out the nuns and destroyed the building. Grant (*Old and New Edinburgh,* vol. 3) gives woodcuts of 1854 showing considerable remains then used as sheep-folds, but by the time he wrote, twenty years later, they were almost all away.

In the seventeenth century the buildings had been used as a burial place for plague victims from the city and this may have given rise to the story that the nuns cared for the diseased who had been put out of the town to die. Probably they did so, although the relief of such plague stricken was more usually undertaken by the monks of such hospitals as St Roque's, which was also on the Boroughmuir.

In addition to the Sciennes, Katherine had a convent founded in her honour in Glasgow by Richard Blackadder about 1503, but apparently it was never built. At Bothwell a chapel to the saint was founded in 1471 by Lord Hamilton; later it became the parish church of Shotts. At Kincardine-in-Fordoun there was also a chapel and annual fair.

Katherine's festival is 29 or 30 April.

D. H. Farmer, *Oxford Dictionary of Saints*, 1978
J. Grant, *Old and New Edinburgh*, 1883

kenneth (or Cainnech to his fellow

Irishmen) was born about 525 in Derry. His father, although a bard, was so poor that it was said that at Kenneth's birth the family had to depend on a wandering cow, which, divinely inspired, stopped outside their cottage and provided milk for the baby. After acting as herd-laddie, Kenneth began his studies at the monasteries of Clonard and Glasnevin under Finian and Mobi. In both communities he was a fellow student of Columba, but when the dreaded yellow plague of 544 hit south Ireland the students fled, Columba to Derry, where he founded the first of his many monasteries in his native county, Kenneth to Wales where he continued his studies under St Cadoc at Llancarfan.

Although credited with the foundation of several Irish monasteries, Kenneth's name is always associated with Aghaboe (cowfield) on the central plain. For our saint's activities in Ireland, his *Life* in the 'Codex Salmanticensis' provides more readable detail than the usual mediaeval 'vitae', and his Scottish movements are supplemented by Adamnan's *Life of Columba* in which he appears several times as a companion and fellow traveller with that saint.

He is commemorated in many Scottish place-names but we must always remember that probably several of these date back only to mediaeval times and need further support before they can be used as evidence of the saint's presence. He was so widely honoured in Fife that he shares with St Serf the honour of being known as the apostle of that kingdom.

Kenneth is linked with Comgall and Columba as approaching Brude, King of the Picts, at Inverness, probably not so much in the hope of converting the king as of trying to secure better facilities for Christian missionaries in Brude's dominions. It has been argued that Kenneth came from one of the Irish tribes which have been called Picts but are now more accurately known as Cruithni, who had some relationship with the Britons. If so he might have been better able to represent the British and Pictish case to Brude than the Gaidheal Columba. His previous sojourn in Wales would have helped him to converse with Britons and Picts in their own tongue, which Columba could not do without an interpreter. Kenneth and Columba were again together, along with Cormac and Brendan, at a concelebrated mass on the little island of Hinba in the Carvelloch Isles which has become known as the 'Mass of the Saints'.

Adamnan relates several incidents involving Kenneth, although as usual he is mainly interested in their miraculous content. On one occasion when a great storm was sweeping down the Sound of Iona, far off in Aghaboe, Kenneth by some feat of divine extra-sensory perception sensed that Columba and his monks urgently needed his prayers and leaving grace unsaid in the refectory he rushed across to the church with one shoe off and the other on. By his immediate and urgent intercession he averted the danger. During another fierce storm on Iona Columba told his monks to prepare for a guest. Although they protested that no traveller could approach the island in such weather, Columba assured them that 'to a certain man who will come to us before evening the Almighty has granted a calm even in the midst of the storm'. The man was, of course, St Kenneth and when he arrived his sailors assured the monks that they had had a calm sea although they had clearly seen the storm in the distance. An instance of forgetfulness was also recorded. When Kenneth was leaving Iona, he left his crozier on the beach. Columba, finding it, carried it to the oratory and remained long in prayer. By then Kenneth was landing on Islay and to his surprise he found the same crozier lying on the turf where it had apparently just been washed up.

Another winter story about Kenneth, told in 'Codex Salmanticensis', tells how, when he was crossing the Dorsum Britanniae, or Highland mountains, he found a woman half-dead with hunger and cold lying in the snow, and beside her a little girl already dead. Ordering his companions to kindle a fire and get some warm food to her, he managed to revive her and also restore her daughter to life. The place, says the writer, was in his day still marked by great crosses— leaving us to interpret it either as specially-erected memorials to the miracle or as indicating that it had taken place near some of the early existing Pictish stones found all over this area. Frank Knight places the incident at the Pass of Glencoe while Pochin Mould envisages it as in the Great Glen.

Kenneth's name is linked with dozens of Scottish churches, chapels and wells although at present there seem only to be two parish churches dedicated to him. Kennoway in Fife is named after him and its old high street, now merely a lane, is still Kenneth's. At St Andrews the early connection with Kenneth has been largely replaced by local legends of St Regulus. Montquhanie, Pitkannie, Ramornie and Strathkinness probably all point to him.

There are Kilchenzies in Ayrshire and Kintyre and a Cill-Chainnich where the parish church of Iona now stands. Off Mull is the island of Inchkenneth which impressed Johnson and Boswell on their Highland tour. There are many Kenneth dedications in the western isles and the Highlands. On the Forth the great mediaeval abbey of Cambuskenneth may be to the saint rather than any of the kings.

Tradition accepts that in his later years Kenneth returned to his parent community of Aghaboe where he died peacefully, ministered to by his younger colleague, St Fintan. The probable date of his death is 600.

His festival is 11 October.

A. O. and M. O. Anderson (eds), *Adomnan's Life of Columba*, 1961

D. Pochin Mould, *The Irish Saints*, 1964

C. Plummer (ed), *Vitae Sanctorum Hiberniae*, 1968

kentigern or mungo

stands second only to Columba among the saints of north Britain in popularity if we reckon the number of fairs, wells, chapels and other places associated with his name in one form or another—Kentigern, Mungo or occasionally the Welsh form Cyndeyrn. The exact meaning in the main forms is involved and somewhat doubtful. 'Kentigernus', from the Gaidhealic, is Latinised in the mediaeval biographer Jocelyn's pages as

'capitalis dominus' or 'head-hound'. The nickname Mungo, most popular among the Cumbrian and Strathclyde Britons, may just mean
'dear beloved' or 'my dear' but it has also a
canine suggestion such as 'my doggie'. (It has
been pointed out that in some way the names
'Kentigern' and 'Mochaoi' are linked, for a
Gaidhealic form of Mungo could become
'Mochua', and the Dumfriesshire parish of Kirk-
mahoe is also connected with Kentigern.)

If we really seek historical truth about this
saint we must put aside the traditional 'biography' of Kentigern which is unfortunately still
being taught, preached and believed in Scotland.
It was pieced together in the later Middle Ages
from a few references in the *Aberdeen Breviary*, a
few fragments from an earlier biography (the
Herbertian) composed for the saint's cathedral at
Glasgow and, chiefly, but least reliably, a 'life'
written (to supplant the older 'life') by Jocelyn of
Furness for a namesake of his who was bishop of
Glasgow. It is seldom realised that the cathedral
founder died not far short of six centuries before
the 'biography'—from which modern anecdotes
and incidents from the saint's life are taken—was
composed. In addition, its author, Jocelyn, confesses that he had suppressed parts of the
original which might have been heretical. His
overriding object was to glorify the see of
Glasgow of which Kentigern had once been
bishop. Jackson has called Kentigern 'the cuck-
oo in the nest' among Celtic 'saints', for parts of
the biographies of other missionaries have been
introduced as his, and doubtful links with other
leading figures, Columba, Serf and the Welsh
David, are put forward as if they were established
facts. It is no easy task, then, to attempt in a few
pages a biography of this figure in whom

folk-myth, legend and real history are all inter-
woven.

In the traditional rendering of Kentigern's life
the scene is set not, as we might imagine, near
Glasgow but in the eastern Lothian area, and
there it is linked to the great Arthurian legendary
cycle through Loth, whom Arthur had made king
of Lothian. In course of time, Loth's daughter,
variously called Enoch, Thenew or, in Welsh,
Denyw, was wooed. When she was found to be
pregnant Loth determined on punishment for his
daughter and she was sent out to sea in an
oarless coracle. In due course the coracle
grounded just downstream from Culross.

Enoch would not reveal the name of the father
of her child, Kentigern, but in time the question
of the child's paternity became such an embar-
rassment to the Church that a rumour arose that
Enoch had conceived miraculously. This was
swiftly denounced as blasphemy by the authorities.

At this point two new figures enter the legend:
one is the baby, Kentigern, born as the Fife coast
was reached; the other is the aged missionary,
Serf (later considered the Apostle of the Ochils)
who stepped forward and undertook the responsibility of fostering the child at his 'muinntir'
close by.

Of Kentigern's boyhood years with Serf at
Culross we know little. Jocelyn did not conceive it
any part of his duty to provide a biography and
we are so much the poorer that the young saint
had no Adamnan at his side. Even the many
miracles recorded seem to lack the freshness and
spontaneity of those attributed to Columcille—
the monastery cook is restored to life as, on
another occasion, is Serf's dead robin, and
Kentigern's progress is marked by a heavenly

effulgence. A selection of these miracles now graces Glasgow's coat-of-arms. Many are taken direct from the mediaeval hagiographer's stock in hand which were used for a number of saints as the occasion required.

All was not harmony, however, at the Culross community. Kentigern, perhaps because he was obviously favoured by the teacher, was resented by his fellows, who made life so difficult, even for a juvenile saint, that he determined to run away to form his own community. In Jocelyn's description, the waters of the Forth divided to let Kentigern through. At Kernach, near Airth, he paused to minister to an aged saint, Fergus, and promised to see to his burial. The body was laid on a bier drawn by two untamed oxen, and was buried when the cart eventually stopped at Cathures (usually taken to be Glasgow) on the site of a cemetery consecrated by St Ninian but never yet used.

Perhaps, under the cloak of legend there are here meaningful allusions to historical incidents to which, so far, we have lost the key. Why otherwise introduce the unknown Fergus at the point of death? Why bring in the future town of Glasgow under a name never again to be used? And, also, difficult to explain, why did Ninian found a cemetery which was not needed for another couple of centuries? Besides, what is entailed in 'founding' a cemetery other than digging the first grave and reading a prayer?

This story has done one necessary thing. It has introduced Kentigern to his diocese ready to begin his real missionary work.

At the time, the legend indicates, there were some few Christians living near Cathures, but most of the land was still pagan. Very unwillingly, because of his youth, Kentigern was persuaded to become their bishop, consecrated, after the Celtic manner, by a single bishop summoned from Ireland. After setting up in Glasgow what Bishop Forbes suggests was a college of Culdees, Kentigern set off on a tour of his diocese. His return to his headquarters was marred by opposition from King Morken and his servant, Cathen, and to escape the king the saint began his extended journey southward through Cumbria and eventually into Wales.

It is important at this point to forget the present political and national divisions of our land. In the saint's day they were quite different. In the western Highlands and islands of Scotland a Dalreadic kingdom was just forming, Gaelic speaking and inhabited by Scots from Ireland. The rest of the Highlands and the eastern parts down to Fife were Pictish, while in the west an allied folk, the Britons, formed a strong kingdom of Strathclyde. Its area varied but at times it stretched south through Cumbria and marched with Welsh territory. Finally, the eastern Lowlands of Scotland and Northumbria formed the kingdom of Lothian. From time to time the divisions regrouped and various smaller units became independent and powerful, for example, Rheged, the area of modern Cumbria and Galloway.

In Kentigern's time, the ruler of the Strathclyde kingdom was Rhydderch with Morken either a sub-ruler or a temporary usurper. As Kentigern moved south to escape the dangers in Strathclyde he crossed the Solway, and left lasting memories of his presence in many villages he passed.

In Cumberland itself no less than eight churches are dedicated to the saint and there are other traditions connected with his work. It is no exaggeration to claim that no district in Scotland holds Kentigern in greater veneration than does the English Lake District. Any unbiassed historian, however, would admit that later mediaeval cults played strange tricks with the original dedications from Celtic times, linking saints to churches in districts where they had never worked and with which they had no previous connections. It is difficult, however, to explain the clusters of Mungo and Kentigern names other than by some more real contact with the saint or his immediate followers. Jackson, not the most credulous of scholars, rejects the saint's Welsh contacts as mainly fictitious but believes in the validity of most of these Cumbrian sites.

We do not know how long Kentigern lingered in Cumbria. Jocelyn may have been reading back more than he should when he described the saint as having to fight against both paganism and heresy. In tradition the saint next moves down to Wales, whose people were in race and language close to the Cumbrians. Jackson believes that, while most of the church dedications in Cumbria arose in mediaeval times, they do represent genuine historic links with Kentigern; the Welsh legends, on the other hand, are accretions to the saint's life and quite legendary. In tradition his Welsh labours resulted in little more permanent than foundations at Llanelwi and Llancarfan.

When eventually Rydderch's power was re-established, Kentigern was invited back to Strathclyde. In fact, the Cumbrian and Welsh expedition, if they ever took place, must have filled Kentigern's itinerary for several years, and meantime one must ask what was happening to the recently founded Strathclyde diocese. Even after his return north, the accounts suggest he spent another eight years lingering in a remote corner of the diocese around Hoddom (Dumfries-shire) before returning to Glasgow.

Of course, it cannot be accepted that Kentigern was ever a diocesan bishop—he was a chorepiscopos or episcopos vagans, a country or travelling bishop without a see or any well defined diocesan jurisdiction.

The focus of Kentigern's labours during the final years of his ministry was so definitely Annandale and the surrounding districts that some scholars consider these to be the original authentic traditions and feel this was where the widespread and powerful cult of Kentigern originated. While dedications to the saint are not found in great numbers in Glasgow and the lower Clyde areas they abound in Annandale and Dumfries-shire and overflow through the adjacent Border counties.

When we glance back over our examination of Kentigern's life we will realise that we have really got little information about him. Many of the dedications come to us only from centuries after his day when, particularly in the ninth and tenth centuries, there was a marked revival of interest in the saint—political influences led to chapels and altars in his honour, but, unlike Columba, there are few details of what he did. The meeting of the two saints recorded by Jocelyn would surely have been mentioned by Adamnan had it really taken place. Most of the miracles in his story are also suspect or are variations of folk-tales.

To study this saint in the cold light of day is to be somewhat disillusioned as one finds oneself in the role of debunker and detective; to visit many of the places in the story and listen to the local folk tell with delight the wonder-working of their saint is to believe again in the childlike, holy

Kentigern who once stood where we stand but who wrought what we could not for lack of faith.

Perhaps by now we will have realised that the real miracle of Kentigern is to be found not in any of the decorations on Glasgow's coat-of-arms but in the saint's own life and preaching—his power to change men. We conclude then with his meeting with Merlin at Drummelzier.

The parish of Drummelzier lies west of Peebles. With its gentle hills, its quiet flowing River Lyne and its kirk of Stobo it seems today too fair a place to be the final haunt and hide-out of the wizard Merlin in his last demented years. Haunted by remorse for his part in the great battle of Arthuret where he had supported the cause of the pagan kings, Merlin, in the northern version of the Arthurian cycle, roamed wild by the woods of Drummelzier where great Tweed meets the little Powsail Burn. To this place came St Kentigern as he journeyed round his favourite country, and there the heathen wizard heard him. The tired heart softened and near that place, by the great stone which folk say was once an altar, the wizard confessed and was baptised. We would rather leave our aged saint there in the forest of Caledon, beside the thorn tree which was to mark the grave of Arthur's wizard, than follow him back to the banks of the Molendinar Burn where he had still, folk say, a few more miracles to perform.

Kentigern's death was around 612, and his festival is 13 January.

K. H. Jackson, *Studies in the Early British Church*, 1958
A. B. Scott, *The Pictish Nation*, 1918

kenτιɣeRna Known to the med-
iaeval hagiologists as 'The Lady of Grace',

Kentigerna might more appropriately be called 'The Lady of The Lake' for she is, or deserves to be, the patron of Loch Lomond, an honour which she might be asked to share with the male St Kessog of Luss.

This little known but very worthy saint of the eighth century was the daughter of Cellach Cualann, King of Leinster, and sister of Comgan who became a missionary in the Loch Alsh district. She married one Feredach or Feriach, who appears to have been rather more fierce and unlovely than the average Celtic ruler of his time, for it was reported that when their son, Faolin or Fillan, was born Feredach took an instant dislike to his appearance and, fearing that the baby might grow up into some misshapen monster, ordered him to be drowned in a nearby lake. Fortunately the story may be discounted for, as is explained elsewhere, it applies to a quite different baby Fillan with a different father.

Feredach and Kentigerna had a numerous family but on the death of the former—a suggested date is 717—she joined her brother Comgan. Taking Fillan with her she left her native country to settle in Scotland in the Loch Alsh district. How long she remained there is not known; perhaps she waited till the death of her brother, who, being of royal blood, was ferried over to the kings' burial ground in Reilig Odhrain. Almost all that we know of Kentigerna's life and work during these years is that she laboured with Comgan and proved to be particularly helpful in cases involving family problems, parental difficulties and such matters, which was natural as she herself had borne a large family.

It must have been at this point that she decided to make a dramatic change in her life style. She turned from the world to become a recluse on the little island opposite Balmaha, then called Kildarie but ever afterwards to be associated with her as Inch-cailleach, Nun's Island. An alternative rendering of the Gaelic would be 'the island of the old woman' and this might fit the picture better, for to those looking from across the water it would indeed be a little old lady whom they would glimpse as she peered out at the sunrise or the sunset on the loch.

In the 1890s the Reverend W. H. Macleod carried out excavations on the island. He found, beneath the debris and vegetation of two and a half centuries, the ruins of a mediaeval church, probably of the twelfth or thirteenth century. It had been the parish church for the little parish of Inch-cailleach. A few dressed arch-stones were enough to suggest the date. This, of course, did not lead him back nearly as far as Kentigerna, but at the east end where once had stood the altar, a stone slab over six feet long still lay and beneath it a number of human bones. With the limited archaeological knowledge of the day Mr Macleod could draw no conclusions, but it seems not unlike the discovery at Ardwall, in the Isles of Fleet, not far short of a century later, where the shrine of an early Christian 'saint' had been transferred to a later oratory of the church. Persisting in his digging, Mr Macleod uncovered what he took to be the ruins of a much earlier, smaller building at the edge of a rock with a spring of clear water nearby. Very likely this would be the cell of Kentigerna.

In 1630 the small parish of Inch-cailleach was united with Buchanan and services were transferred to the mainland. The new church, opened in 1764, was destroyed by fire in 1938 when the ancient font from the island was destroyed but the bell was saved. Mentioning the old graveyard on the island the *Third Statistical Account* records the last island burial as 1947.

Kentigerna is remembered at Kilkinterna (Cill-Chaointearn) in Glenshiel. She is often spelled Quentigerna.

Her festival is 7 January.

D. H. Farmer, *Oxford Dictionary of Saints*, 1978

kessog

For many years travellers driving north from Inverness have suffered the frustration of having to face the diversion westward to go round the head of the Beauly Firth to reach the Black Isle. The beautiful but time-consuming diversion will soon be bypassed by the bridge over the firth, and then the famous or infamous Kessock Ferry will run no more.

The name is that of St Kessog or Makessog, a sixth century Irish saint or missionary, said, like all such, to be of the Munster royal family at Cashel. His missionary work was almost entirely in Scotland, especially around Loch Lomond where he is commemorated at Monk's Island and is patron of Luss, having links with the Clan Colquhoun. His pre-Reformation image was kept at Rossdhu and his bell reverenced in Lennox up to the seventeenth century. An annual fair in his honour was held at Callander and a similar one on Cumbrae. Tradition alleges he was martyred, one version stating this happened in a foreign land after which the body, wrapped in sweet herbs, was brought back to Loch Lomondside and buried at Luss (in Gaelic 'luss' means herb).

His festival is 13 January or 10 March.

D. H. Farmer, *Oxford Dictionary of Saints*, 1978
A. P. Forbes, *Kalendars of Scottish Saints*, 1872

ꞁꜲURENCE The most famous of the four canonised saints of this name was the third-century Roman Christian who was martyred and whose symbol is a grid-iron. But it is a later namesake, Laurentius of Canterbury, assistant and successor to St Augustine, whom we describe here and who is commemorated by having a whole Scottish town, even if quite a small one, named after him.

Laurence appears in Bede's history as the rather autocratic and condescending bishop of the English Churchmen who accused the British and Welsh bishops of schism—dates of the observance of festivals and some details of ritual differed from those accepted by the main body of the western, more Romanised Church. Bede himself had no doubt at all that Christ and his angels were firmly behind the new arrivals at Canterbury—Augustine, Laurence, Mellitus, Justus and the rest of the party from Rome. But there always has been a contrary point of view, expressed most loudly north of the Border.

Perhaps the strongest argument against Augustine's view that the only true or Catholic version of the faith lay with the continental usages is that the British Christians had enjoyed a fully organised Church, with no hint of heresy. It was natural that after centuries of physical and cultural separation differences should have arisen, and so, unfortunately, insular pride and appeal to ancient tradition on one side faced appeal to universal custom on the other. The British bishop Dagan refused to sit at the table with Laurence—but that might well have been only because it was one of his fast days. Augustine did not rise at the approach of the Britons—but it might not have been the continental custom for an archbishop to do so.

After much talk, the two parties went their separate ways and kept their own customs. Today you may drive over the great Severn Bridge and look down on the roofs of the village of Aust below you—the scene, tradition says, of that momentous conference. Neither there nor in the nearby town of Chepstow have many heard of that meeting of the bishops, but worshippers still take their separate ways—some to follow a service Augustine might have appreciated and shared in, others to follow a simpler kind of service which the British bishops would have understood.

Of course, there was more to it than that. The British did not really want much to do with the wild English who had murdered their brothers; the English viewed the Britons as barbarous, wild folk, only partly civilised. It is perhaps no coincidence that Laurencekirk is the only dedication to this English-orientated bishop, but it is strange that only a few miles away is the traditional grave of St Palladius who was contemporary with St Patrick and who probably represented a Westernised-Romanised interpretation of the faith which both sides might have understood.

Laurence's festival is 3 February.

D. Attwater, *Penguin Dictionary of Saints,* 1965

B. Colgrave and R. A. B. Mynors (eds), *Bede: Historia Ecclesiastica,* 1969

Leonard

In his youth St Leonard was a nobleman at the court of King Clovis I of the Franks. He was converted to the faith by St Remigius of Rheims and under his influence gave up palace life and retired to the monastery of Micy near Orleans. Seeking still deeper seclusion he became a hermit, building himself an oratory in a forest near Limoges. His sanctity attracted others to join him and they formed the nucleus of the future Benedictine monastery of Noblat.

His patron, Clovis, died while Leonard was still a young monk. His successor, Theodebart, who used to go hunting near the oratory, was on one occasion accompanied by the queen, Misigard, when she was suddenly overtaken by the pains of childbirth. Apparently Leonard officiated as midwife, for when she was safely delivered of a child the saint was offered as much land as he could ride round in one night on an ass—a grant which provided enough land for the growing monastery.

From his youth Leonard had displayed special interest in the plight of prisoners and captives, of whom there were many in those troubled days. It was said that Clovis made a promise to release any for whom Leonard made special petition. In art he is usually shown carrying fetters or chains and he is considered the patron of prisoners— also of midwives and expectant mothers. The church on the site of the monastery of Noblat claims to possess the saint's skull and some of his bones.

The cultus of Leonard became popular in Britain after the return of the crusaders, many of whom had themselves had unhappy experiences of prisons. In Scotland he was patron of several 'hospitals', places of sojourn for the streams of pilgrims to holy places, of retreat for the aged and of healing for the sick. Of these, three were especially notable.

At St Andrews, as the number of pilgrims diminished in the fifteenth century, the buildings became almshouses for aged women. There were complaints about women's conduct and so, in 1512, the buildings were converted by Archbishop Stuart and Prior Hepburn into a college for poor clerks. This became St Leonard's College. This college, it has been said, grew out of the decline in faith. Although intended as a bastion for orthodoxy it became the breeding place for reformation—'to drink of St Leonard's well' meant heresy. In 1747 when the decay of the nation as the result of the Act of Union of forty years earlier was being severely felt, St Leonard's and St Salvator's Colleges were united and the old chapel of St Leonard's disused. Today the remains of the college, much altered and used by a girls' school and by the university, still form what one scholar describes as 'the most nearly complete group of Scottish mediaeval college edifices'.

For over a century the college chapel lay in ruins. When Dr Johnson visited it he complained that it had 'been converted into a kind of greenhouse . . . this experiment is unsuccessful, the plants do not hitherto prosper'—doubtless because flat mediaeval tombstones lay beneath two feet of earth on which they were planted. Last century Andrew Lang wrote of it:

O ruined chapel! Long ago
We loitered where the tall
Fresh budded mountain ashes blow
Within thy desecrated wall.

Today it is reconsecrated and regularly used for student services. Approached through the

Pends and the ancient gateway the environs offer a quiet corner; inside, with its great painting of Leonard and its mediaeval tombs, the atmosphere is altogether worthy.

In Edinburgh, St Leonard's Hospital provided care for half a dozen aged men until the moneys disappeared into the purses of nobles and burghers at the Reformation. The district, immortalised by Scott in *The Heart Of Midlothian,* was known as Mount Hooly and stood at the boundary of the Boroughmuir on the steep western scarp of the Queen's Park. About 1854, when the area was completely built over with tenements, all traces of hospital and chapel disappeared except for a few fragments beneath a public house at the corner of St Leonard's Lane and St Leonard's Hill. These streets are once again cleared, but it seems unlikely that there has been anything left to be uncovered.

The Dunfermline St Leonard's Hospital or Hospice was situated in the lower part of the town beside the road to Queensferry, where now stands a primary school bearing the saint's name. It seems to have been quite an attractive foundation with a separate room and small garden for each of eight old ladies. At the Reformation it suffered the fate of all similar charities, its moneys being quickly appropriated. The record of 1 April 1651 reads, 'Ane supplication being presented by James Esplin, Elymosinar of the Hospital of St Leonard, situate beside the burgh of Dunfermline, for himself and in name of the widows thereof, desyring the charity of the several Presbyteries for re-edifying of the said hospital.' In the same year the hospital chapel was wrecked by 'several rough cavillers'. Bones were exposed on the site of the hospital cemetery in 1890. Its well still remains.

Among other Scottish dedications to the saint are Lanark, Ayr, Lauder, Kinghorn and Perth. Leonard's festival is 6 November.

S. Baring-Gould and J. Fisher, *Lives of the British Saints*, 1913
J. Grant, *Old and New Edinburgh*, 1883
R. Kirk, *St Andrews*, 1954

Llolan All details of the work of this early missionary have perished although, until a century after the Reformation, the Earls of Perth (as 'dewars') preserved his bell and 'bachail' at Kincardine on Forth, and there is a tradition that an ancient bell in Kelvingrove museum was Llolan's. He was said to have been a younger disciple of St Serf, but this may well have been an attempt to regularise his ordination as it was generally accepted that Serf had been ordained by Palladius. Broughton and the Tweed valley hold legends and traditions of Llolan, and the old church of Broughton has a very early monk's cell, traditionally his. It was restored by the architect James Grieve in 1926, has a cross design on the floor, a stained glass window and is turf roofed. Broughton Fair used to be held on the saint's day. Dates for the saint are quite uncertain, but if a connection with Serf is accepted he could be late sixth century.

His festival is 22 September.

the
Macdonald
maidens

Were we forced to confine
ourselves to well-documented facts and to people
whose historicity is above challenge, then neither these young women, worthy as were their
lives, nor their father, Donald or Donevaldus,
would merit any place in these pages. Saints,
however, demand a dispensation of their own,
although this does not mean that we accept and
repeat the miracle stories of mediaeval hagiographers.

In the case of Donevaldus, however, and
others like him, oral tradition has so mixed their
stories in with those of other people who lived in
other places that we must either refuse to give
them any place or set down the most probable
account of their lives.

The basic elements in this story of Donald of
Glen Ogilvie place him in the eighth century. It is
suggested that he was a cleric adhering to the
Celtic Church customs, for by the rule of Rome
by that date celibacy was imposed and the
presence of even one daughter would have
barred him from sainthood. Perhaps it was their
father's example of prolific child-begetting or
perhaps memories of a home too full of greeting
bairns, but all the daughters (in one version nine
in number; in other versions only seven) grew up
determined to preserve their virginity, and did so
in spite of various difficulties.

The names of only three of these Macdonald
maidens have come down to us, and these from

different parts of the country. Mayoca, or St Maik, was said to be the eldest and she is remembered in Aberdeenshire. The parish of Drumoak has its St Maik's Well and various local place-names contain traces of her activities. The sister Fincana becomes St Fink, and is known at Bendochy near Blairgowrie, at Echt and at Alyth. The third maid whose name survives is Fyndoca who is linked with her sister Fincana at Mill of Gask and is remembered herself much further away on Loch Awe and at Killonaig on Mull. In various places they are commemorated together as The Nine Maidens.

The centre of their missionary activity seems to have been around Abernethy on Tay, although the origin of their legend is about the Sidlaws and the parish of Glamis. The most exciting version is that which makes Donevaldus the farmer of Pitempton in Strathmartine parish who was plagued by a fierce dragon. Each day he sent one of his nine daughters out to draw water but eight fell victim to the beast's appetite for human flesh. Then came a Christian knight, Martin, who on the ninth day volunteered to fight the dragon. The battle was at Baldragon and of course Martin won and the menace was removed.

Underlying the ridiculous parts of this legend is the picture of the Christian truth suppressing pagan superstition—and in this case Martin is a real person and no imaginary figure. Surely, however, two or more legends have been intertwined into one composite story. We meet another version in one of the original names for Edinburgh, Castrum Puellarum, Maiden Castle, which again has become linked with the name of a much later figure, Medina or Modwenna. The Nine Maidens' story took them from the Sidlaws

to Tayside at Abernethy and then up the river to
Dunfallandy where some say they died.

A. P. Forbes, *Kalendars of Scottish Saints,* 1872
G. A. F. Knight, *Archaeological Light on the Early
Christianising of Scotland,* 1933

ɱᴀᴄʜᴀʀ St Machar (Machor, Mach-

arius, Mauritius, Mochonnan or Mochrieba)
would not normally deserve any mention in our
pages, as what little is known of him is so riddled
with myth and historical incongruity as to be
almost worthless. However, in deference to the
prestige of the great cathedral which retains him
as patron we give an abbreviation of the fifteenth-
century manuscript poem in Scots vernacular in
Cambridge University library. This, with the
Aberdeen Breviary and Colgan's *Fifth Life of
Columba,* includes all that is known about
Machar, and the material all derives from a late
Life in Latin. In addition to a number of stock
mediaeval miracles and a few original ones, it
gives few historical incidents which are not open
to challenge.

Machar was born in Ireland of princely parentage and at his birth angels sang round his
cradle. He early showed miraculous powers by
restoring his dead brother to life through sleep-
ing in the same bed. He joined the great
Columba and crossed in the first coracle with the
original party to Iona, but as his outstanding
sanctity roused the jealousy of the other saints he
left to work on Mull and eventually moved east to
found a new community at a place where,
Columba had advised him, he would find a river
bending in the shape of a crozier. This, of course,
he found at the spot on the River Don where the
mediaeval cathedral was later built. Machar was

friends with the missionaries Devenick and Ter-
nan, who both had their 'bangors' or 'bancories'
(missionary centres) in the neighbourhood. Columba asked Machor to accompany him to Rome
and on the return journey they left him to stay at
Tours as bishop, an appointment recommended
by the ghost of St Martin who reappeared for the
occasion. At Machar's death Martin flew down
from heaven to be present; Columba also flew
over to Aberdeen from Iona and a numerous host
from heaven attended. It would be unnecessary
to outline which sections of this remarkable
biography should be considered legendary.

After throwing doubt on the traditional 'life' we
must stand in admiration of the great cathedral
in Old Aberdeen which honours his memory. It is
one of the few cathedrals which still stands
surrounded by its own village, or 'chanonry', little
altered since mediaeval times. A lesser example
may be seen at Fortrose.

The saint is remembered at Old and New
Machar, Kildrummy (Macharshaugh), near
Aboyne (the cross of St Mochrieha and
Muchrieha's chair and well), Macharmuir and
Macharford near Newburgh-on-Ythan. In Gaelic
'machar' signifies a tract of moorland and this
might account for the place-names.

If we discount the Columban connections we
might see him as one of the Celtic missionaries
evangelising near the mouth of the Don.

His festival is 12 November.

maelꞅuꞇha, 'the red priest', was
one of the most important missionaries of the
early British Church and deserves fuller recognition than has been accorded him in the past.
Looking north from Strome Ferry on the Kyle

railway to the Applecross peninsula and the towering mountains of Loch Torridon (one of Scotland's most magnificent vistas), we are viewing Maelrubha's adopted country:

Into Scotland with purity
after leaving every happiness
went our brother Maelrubha.

Thus sang the Irish poet Oengus in his *Felire*. This corner of Scotland, although geographically not as far north as Inverness, was until recently remote and little known, but now oil developments at Loch Kishorn and Loch Carron have given it new importance and it is appropriate that in the archaeological world the excavations at Maelrubha's Applecross 'muinntir' have excited fresh interest in the saint.

Born near Derry in 642, Maelrubha was eighth in direct line of descent from the famous Irish adventurer, Niall of the Nine Hostages, who had himself been responsible (if tradition be correct) for the capture and enslavement of St Patrick. He was, therefore, although in time a century later, a cousin to Columba. On the maternal side he came of Pictish stock and therefore combined the blood of the two great branches of the Celts which at that time were in rivalry in Alba (Scotland). As a young man he became a member of the great monastic community of Bangor (Ulster) but about 671, when he was approaching thirty, he followed the Irish monks' practice of cutting himself off from his homeland and choosing a foreign land in which to go wandering for Christ.

After two years' missionary work round the north-west of Scotland he settled in the remote peninsula of Apercrossan, where, with many excursions to found daughter churches in these mountainous glens and islands, he remained until his death in 722 at the advanced age of eighty. A contrary tradition suggested that the saint was martyred during one of the first invasions of the 'Black Gentiles' (Danes) in Strathnaver where a rough stone is said to mark his grave. There is no record of his ever revisiting his native Ireland.

Although Maelrubha is more certainly an historic figure than many Celtic saints, attempts to trace his missionary movements from the many place-names which appear to commemorate him still present many difficulties. Because the Gaelic language always seeks to achieve euphony, and also because it often prefixes a 'mo' or 'ma' ('my dear'), many variations are legitimate which puzzle the non-Gaelic scholar. For example, St Adamnan can become Skeulan, or Arnold. Bishop Reeves, the century-old authority on Maelrubha, gives no less than thirty-nine variant forms, including Mareve, Moruby, Maree, Arrow, Rufus, Summeruff and Samareve. Some of these forms approximate closely to that of the Blessed Virgin so that in some cases it is impossible to state definitely if a place-name derives from 'the red priest' or from Mary, to whom an increasing number of mediaeval dedications were made. A case in point is the little isolated chapel and graveyard at Kilmory Knap by the side of Loch Sween, still displaying one of the most splendid of later Celtic crosses. Most books take it that the reference is to the Virgin, but it is within our saint's territory and more probably derives from him.

A third cause for confusion is the similarity between the name of the saint and that of an old Celtic god—Mourie. 'Gradually after his death,' writes Frank Knight, 'tradition began to play havoc with his name; so much did his fame increase that in later centuries he was worshipped as the god Mourie.' A minute of a presbytery meeting held at Applecross in 1656 alleges that 'among abominale and heathinishe practizes' on the saint's festival day in that place bulls were sacrificed, and there were approaches to 'some ruinous chappells and circulating of them', and predictions of future events were made by a round stone with a hole into which 'they tryed the entering of thair head'. Again, as late as 1678 certain people were accused by Dingwall presbytery of sacrificing a bull on Innis Maree 'for the recovering of health of Cirstane Mackenzie who was formerly sick and valetudinarie'.

The sacrificing of a bull was surely a pre-Christian pagan custom which had through time become attached to the religious procession round the church and precincts on the saint's day, while the absurd custom of the parishioners sticking their heads through the hollow stone to ascertain their future (not unlike the Blarney Stone) was simply a superstition derived from ancient folk custom. Dr Pochin Mould, however, believed the stories of bulls being sacrificed was a garbled account, given to the presbytery, of the normal meal which would accompany a saint's festival.

In mediaeval times the land for six miles round Applecross was privileged ground, and today in Gaelic the parish is A'Chomraich, the sanctuary. In Muckairn parish, between Oban and Loch Etive, is Kilvary, a possible dedication to our saint, with Ballindeor, the homestead of the 'dewar' (keeper). His duty was to guard a relic which is called in the year 1518 'Arwachyll', an obvious adaptation of 'bachail', the bishop's crook, which probably was the original staff of Maelrubha, preserved in an elaborate silver case.

151

Although one or two relics remain from the days of the saints, this particular crook disappeared, probably at the Reformation.

Dedications to 'the red priest' are so numerous north and west of the Great Glen that only a selection can be mentioned (remembering that some may be a confusion with the Virgin Mary). East of the Glen there are suggested isolated sites at Keith, Fordyce, Forres and Rafford and, further south and more suspicious, at Crail, Kinnell and Amulree. On Islay is Kilarrow, on Skye at Ashaig are Tobar Ma-Rui and Creag-na-Leabhair, where Maelrubha is said to have sat to read the gospels while his bell hung on a nearby tree. On Harris St Maelrubha's was by Loch Seaforth. On the mainland he was remembered at Eilean-Ma-Ruibhe. Innis Maree had an ancient chapel to him, while Urquhart, Contin, Lochcarron and Lairg also all claim connections. In fact, there are few parishes in north-west Scotland which do not commemorate 'the red priest'.

His festival is 21 April or 22 August.

D. Pochin Mould, *The Irish Saints*, 1964

W. D. Simpson, *The Celtic Church in Scotland*, 1935

C. Thomas, *The Early Christian Archaeology of North Britain*, 1972

magnus

The conversion of Earl Sigurd and the Orkney people to Christianity may be dated exactly to the year 995, for in that year King Olaf returned from England to Norway, stopping on the way to meet his subject, the Earl of Orkney, and full of enthusiasm about the new faith into which he had just been baptised. He gave Sigurd and the islanders the choice of immediate mass baptism or death by the swords of his Vikings, and took away the earl's son as hostage for the sincerity of their conversion.

It is against this primitive and bloodthirsty background that a century later we find the first Orcadian saint, Magnus Erlingsson or Erlindson, whose story is recounted in the *Orkneyinga Saga*. About the end of the eleventh century the Orkney earldom was jointly held by cousins— Hakon Paulson and Erling and Magnus Erlingsson. King Magnus Bareknees took all three young earls with him on his raids in Ireland, the Isle of Man and Wales. At a fierce battle in the Menai Straits Erling was killed, leaving the cousins Hakon and Magnus to divide the Orkneys between them. In the battle, however, Magnus had refused to fight and stood aside, chanting psalms—a pacific gesture unlikely to endear him to the Viking king. As a result he left his ship, fled to the woods and eventually to the Scottish court where he sought protection.

On the death of Bareknees, Hakon was proclaimed earl, but Magnus returned to claim his share of the islands. For a few years the cousins reigned uneasily together, but his cousin's fear and dislike of war roused Hakon's anger, especially when Magnus left the islands a second time and went south to pay Henry I of England a year-long visit. When he did return, with five ships and well-armed crews, Hakon, determined that dual rule must end, made quiet but careful plans to have his cousin removed.

A conference was arranged for Easter 1116 on the island of Egilsay, each earl to attend with two ships and an equal number of retainers. Magnus appeared first with the agreed ships and men but soon Hakon was seen approaching with eight ships fully manned for battle. Magnus now knew his fate and retired to the little church to pray and seek 'sanctuary'—the saga reads 'not for fear's sake but to commit to God all his case'. At first light, when the protection of sanctuary ended, Hakon's men rushed into the church only to find it empty. There is some confusion in the old documents at this point, for a martyr was supposed to advance boldly to his death without revealing any fear. The truth is probably that Magnus made an attempt to hide, but finding it impossible came out and made some attempt to bargain with his cousin. If Hakon let him go south to Rome or Jerusalem he would swear never to return. When this was refused he suggested he would go as prisoner to Scotland and be kept confined for the rest of his life. This also was rejected and Magnus finally said, 'One choice then is left; God knows I look more to thy soul than to mine own life. Let me be maimed in my limbs or pluck out mine eyes and set me in a dark dungeon.' Hakon would have accepted this but his followers rejected the idea of torturing an earl and demanded death. In the end it was Hakon's cook, Lifolf, who acted as executioner. When Magnus had prayed he said, 'Stand thou before me and hew me on the head a great wound for it beseems not to chop off a chief's head like thieves'.' 'He signed himself with the cross and bowed himself for the stroke and his spirit passed into heaven.'

Magnus was not strictly a martyr, witnessing for the faith, for Hakon also claimed to be a Christian and for a time many of the bishops inclined to his side. Stories of the dead earl and of miracles attributed to his intervention grew rapidly and just over twenty years after his death his nephew Rognvald prepared to build the great church—now Kirkwall cathedral—to shelter his remains. The bones were removed after the

murder from Egilsay church to Birsay, then to St
Olaf's church at Kirkwall before their final
resting place in the cathedral. The sagas had
portrayed Magnus as 'a tall man of growth, quick
and gallant and strong of body, fair to look on,
light-hued and fair-limbed, noble in aspect.'
When the remains were exhumed and examined
in this century, however, they revealed a man
about five feet seven, not powerful and with a
small skull capacity which suggested no great
intelligence. The great cleft in the skull exactly
corroborated the legend. He was, it would appear,
a man of peaceful nature, retiring and somewhat
timid, quite unsuited to face the duties of leadership if they involved war and bloodshed. His
people so little understood him that they put a
sword in the hand of his effigy in the cathedral,
and in their sagas drew him with the physical
aspects of a powerful Viking, which he was not.
Had he lived today he might have been a
member of the Fellowship of Reconciliation,
perhaps even of the CND. The physical fear of
pain and death was obviously far greater to him
than to so many other martyrs, so any heroism
he did show was so much the nobler. History,
even of those war-like Viking days, should have
some place for those who saw no heroism in
senseless killing. Would that this Magnus had
been able to find some niche in a monastic
cloister.

There are few traces of devotion to Magnus on
the Scottish mainland. Dundee parish church
had an altar to him. In Caithness, Banniskirk
near Spittal may be a corruption of his name,
and the church at Watten and a chapel at
Shebster commemorated him. On the Shetland
mainland he had four dedications and one on
Yell. The ancient church at Egilsay was dedi-

cated to him after the martyrdom and the present building may date from that time. His great memorial is Kirkwall cathedral, the masonry of which shows close links with Durham whose masons probably came north to help in its construction. In addition to the graves of Magnus (found in a wooden coffin) and Rognvald, several croziers of lead and oak were unearthed and are considered to have been copies of more costly croziers which were designed to be buried with the bishops whose real staffs were then passed to their successors.

The most notable dedication in England is the city of London's St Magnus the Martyr, at the edge of the river. There is evidence, however, that it originally referred to an earlier Magnus, for there was there a St Magnus church as early as 1067.

A prayer to St Magnus deserves quotation:

> O Magnus of my love, thou it is who would guide us; thou fragrant body of grace, remember us. Remember us, thou saint of power, who didst encompass and protect the people . . . Lift our flocks to the hills, quell the wolf and the fox, ward from us, spectre, giant, fury and oppression.

The saint's day is 16 April.

malachy was one of that small group

of devout Cistercian friends who had such a cleansing and invigorating influence on the Church about the middle of the twelfth century. The group was represented in Britain by Aelred and in Ulster by Malachy, and they looked to St Bernard of Clairvaux as their leader. Malachy left his vestments to Bernard who thereafter always wore his stole to mass. In both Britain and Ireland the Church badly needed cleansing. When he became bishop of Down, Malachy succeeded eight predecessors not one of whom was in clerical orders and most of whom were married. For two centuries the see of Armagh had been in the hands of members of one family and naturally there was concerted opposition to any alteration in the system. Malachy's undoubted ability, however, in the end secured his preferment to the see of Armagh, the primacy of Ireland.

His connection with Scotland which secures him a brief mention in our notes consisted of two brief visits. However, they were of importance as he took the opportunity to found the first Scottish Cistercian abbey, Soulseat, in the Rinns of Galloway. Sited beside a small, green algae-infested lake it was known as Viride Stagnum but also took the more pleasant title of Sedes Animarum—in English, Soulseat. No other Scottish abbey has suffered such physical destruction, for scarcely one stone remains upon another.

There is some mystery about the history of this abbey for while all the other Cistercian houses (all founded just after or about the same date as Soulseat) flourished and established themselves with their own communities, we lose sight of Soulseat for some years and then find it a house not of Cistercians but of the rival Premonstratensians. It is possible that the Premonstratensians and not Malachy founded Soulseat. Unfortunately, we would then be left with one surplus abbey, site unknown, unrecorded and undiscovered.

Malachy's festival is 3 November.

B. Scott, *Malachy*, 1976.

MARGARET and her husband Malcolm Canmore were strangely assorted bed-

mates. Margaret, a Saxon–Hungarian princess, daughter of Edward the Atheling and grand-daughter of King Edmund Ironside, was pious, devout, even saintly. Malcolm Canmore was a fiery Celtic ruffian, already married to an older princess who conveniently disappears from history about this time. When he first met his young bride Malcolm was down at Wearmouth burning the Saxon church and slaughtering young and old indiscriminately. Margaret's royal party was in flight from England and her new Norman conquerors and perhaps they were headed for the continent when a chance storm drove them to the Northumbrian coast. It is just possible that the couple had met before, for Malcolm had been a refugee at the English court and was leaving to assume the Scottish throne when the child Margaret, another refugee, arrived. 'If Malcolm ever saw Margaret,' writes Rosalind Masson, 'he saw a demure little maiden who, having been brought up rigorously at the pious court of Hungary, now found herself in the equally pious but more ceremonious court of Edward the Confessor, where she and her sister were handed over to the care of a "Mistress of Maidens". And if dignified little Margaret ever saw Malcolm, she saw a tall Celt twice her age.'

The boat-load of royal refugees made no further attempt to go nearer the continent, if they had ever intended to go there, but followed the king of Scots to his royal tower. Today one may stand within the stump of it, the Dun-ferm-line— the fort by the twisty burn—and visualise the young princess and her retinue approaching from Rosyth to greet the monarch, eleven years her senior, whom very shortly she was to marry. On

his side it was a political affair, uniting him to the
royal Saxon line, but it seems soon to have
become a love-match too, for Malcolm was
always gentle and understanding with his young
wife: 'he readily obeyed her wishes and prudent
counsels in all things; whatever she refused, he
refused also; whatever pleased her, he also loved
for love of her' (Turgot, her confessor). On her
side one must doubt whether any deep affection
could have been involved, but all considerations
demanded that she must wed or else remain all
her life under a succession of 'Mistresses of
Maidens'—and where was there another so
eligible young prince? Her pleas to retire to live in
cloistered seclusion did not greatly impress her
advisers and perhaps she herself in the end
realised that here was a God-given chance to
influence King Malcolm and at the same time
bring his nation into full acceptance of the
western Catholic Church of which she was such
a devout protagonist.

All this Margaret in the end achieved by a
mixture of personal saintliness, political tact and
ecclesiastical sagacity in a way no Church courts
or Church dignitaries could have done. The old
'Celtic' Church with its distinctive customs and
individualistic ways was in any case in decay; the
Culdees—Cele Dei (usually taken to mean 'God
seekers' but possibly coming from an old Irish
word for 'the Strange Ones')—were in retreat
before the disciplined and dignified Roman clergy. Margaret included a Culdee among her
marriage signatories, but rapidly began the
transformation to Norman customs and continental ways, aided and encouraged by her
confessor; the illustrious Prior Turgot of Durham,
and Lanfranc, Archbishop of Canterbury.

She rebuilt her home church of Dunfermline,

the first of a long series of enlargements and extensions which continued into last century. No trace of the Culdee church was left but beneath the gratings in the floor of the nave the outlines of her foundations may be seen today. Here she introduced into Scotland for the first time the monastic order of Benedictines, making Dunfermline a daughter house from Canterbury. Her son, Edgar, followed his mother's pious example by staffing Coldingham from Durham. Another of the royal sons, Alexander I, introduced Augustinian canons to Scone and then to St Andrews. David, her sixth son, continued monastic foundations, with Tironensians, Clunaic, Premonstratensians and Cistercians, and by the time of his death in 1153 the structure of the Church in Scotland was the internationally-accepted pattern of cathedrals and abbeys with dependent parishes clustered around.

Margaret held to her private prayers and devotions, reading from her Evangelistarium, the little illuminated gospel which Scotland allowed to pass out of her hands but which is prized today by the Oxford Bodleian. The cell which was her retreat has recently disappeared under the tarmac of a car-park, although the visitor is advised that a key to the rusty padlock may be obtained on request.

Margaret was in Edinburgh castle when death approached, and she took her last communion in chapel—the little stone chapel, we like to think, or if not, then a slightly earlier version which she had built on the castle rock. Malcolm, as so often, was away fighting in England. At the battle of Alnwick both he and Edward, their eldest son, were mortally wounded. The fourth son, Edgar, rode to Edinburgh with the news. Margaret had been borne back to her chamber and was holding the black cross which she had brought with her from England. When tidings of the tragedy were passed to her, she died.

Moves for the beatification of Margaret were made by Abbot de Keldeleth about 1250. He was a clever but ambitious cleric who realised that the heavy cost of repairing and maintaining a great building like the abbey at Dunfermline was only possible if there was in it the shrine of a saint which would draw crowds of pilgrims with their generous gifts. During his abbacy strange miracles were reported at the queen's tomb: passersby saw lights and sparks which must surely be signs of her unrecognised sanctity and applications were quickly made to Rome for beatification. Andrew Wyntoun writes in his *Orygnale Cronykil*:

> That yeir with veneratioun
> Was maid the translatioun
> Of Sainct Margret the haly quene;
> A fair miracle thair was sein.

To move Margaret to a shrine behind the high altar would leave her rather worldly spouse blocking the nave in assymetrical isolation and so it was fortunate that the saint's coffin refused to be moved forward until Malcolm was carried up beside her:

> Her cors they tuik up, and bair ben,
> And thaim interrit togeder then.
> Swa trowit all they that gadderit thair
> Quhat honour til her lord she bair.

Margaret, now saint and queen, lay in her gilded shrine till the Reformation, when the last abbot, George Durie, hid her relics at his nearby estate of Craiglusker till they could be smuggled to France where later they disappeared in the Revolution. The new Protestant church occupied the former nave and the great choir with the shrine became ruinous. In the nineteenth century it in turn became the parish church, but in the rebuilding the east wall was so contrived that the blank stone slab where the shrine of the lady saint had stood was left outside at the mercy of the elements, remembered not at all by the majority of the citizens and by the minority, successors of the mediaeval order which was so dear to Margaret's heart, once only each year at a pilgrimage and picnic.

The place of Margaret's first landing in Scotland is known as St Margaret's Hope and directly across the Firth is Port Edgar, recalling the Aetheling. Queensferry was, of course, named after her and the seal of the former burgh shows the queen about to land from a boat. Dunfermline remembers her in several place-names while Edinburgh castle was long protected by a St Margaret's tower and gate. Her well is still at the foot of the rock. Beyond Holyrood is St Margaret's Loch while a more modern memorial (now demolished) was the busy St Margaret's locomotive shed. The parishes of Urquhart in Moray, Forgue in Aberdeenshire and the suppressed parish of Abercrombie, near St Monans, Fife, were in her patronage. Even in the later Middle Ages, after she had been beatified, churches in her honour were not many, because parishes clung to the names of saints of the old Celtic Church, or because they followed the Roman habit of apostolic dedications. The *Survey Gazetteer* of 1950 lists five Scottish parishes in her name, but all are 'quoad sacra' and therefore recent; they are in Edinburgh, Dundee, Govan, Hawick and Arbroath. The Roman Catholic directory lists twenty churches honouring this saint while the Church of Scotland has ten.

A vision of Margaret is supposed to have appeared before the Battle of Largs in support of the Scottish army and in that town there is a Margaret's Law. Forfar had a manor, well and inch named for her; Dundee had an old 'land' and a close in the Overgate. There were altars in St Giles, Edinburgh, and Dundee. Most of the many Margaret dedications in England, Ireland and elsewhere apply to a much earlier Margaret, the martyr of Antioch.

Her festival is 16 November.

R. Masson, *Scotland: The Nation*, 1934

marnock or ernene

Such are the complexities and permutations of the Gaelic language that Marnock and Ernene are one and the same person. There are over twenty-five Ernans, Ernenes, or Ernines in the Irish kalendars of saints, including an uncle and a nephew of St Columba; but it is reasonably safe to identify the Marnock who is remembered in our Scottish town and in many place-names with Ernene or Mernog of Rathnew in Co. Wicklow, who receives a chapter to himself in Adamnan's *Life of Columba*.

The incident recorded by Adamnan occurred during a visit by Columba to the monastery of Clonmacnois in 585—for, contrary to belief, the saint did revisit Ireland in the later years of his life. The ancient monastery, although changed and added to in mediaeval times, still stands today, lonely and lovely, beside the broad, silent-flowing Shannon. Alitherus, the fourth abbot since the foundation of Clonmacnois by St Kieran, determined to give his illustrious visitor full honours and Adamnan presents us with a

163

vivid technicolour pen-picture of the procession which wound its way past the oratories and cells to the church—now called Temple Kieran—with Columba protected by four bearers holding aloft a rich canopy on poles while other ushers kept back the throngs of brethren, for such communities sometimes housed more than a thousand inmates and the saint was frail and advanced in years.

In the midst of this solemn procession a small boy was discovered hiding under the canopy and holding on to the edge of the saint's long cloak—the woolly Irish 'casail'—which he was wearing. As the lad was dragged away there were cries of 'Pack him off! Away with the naughty little urchin!' Columba, who had already sensed that someone was touching him, put his hand to the boy's face and, looking at him, said quietly, 'Son, open your mouth and put out your tongue.' When young Marnock did so, Columba upbraided the crowd for despising the boy and prophesied, 'He will increase in good conduct and the virtues of the soul, and great will be his progress in this your community. His tongue also shall be gifted by God with wholesome doctrine and eloquence.'

This simple story bears every evidence of truth, and Adamnan goes on to say that the boy himself, later in life, told it to Abbot Seghine (Adamnan's predecessor) in the presence of a monk, Failbhe, who passed it to Adamnan. O'Hanlon suggested that the lad continued his education at Clonmacnois under Alitherus and then moved east to found the church at Rathnew, north-west of Wicklow. There are no means of knowing when he sailed to continue his missionary activities in Scotland, but it was the accepted thing for an Irish monk of his day to go wandering for Christ's sake. The only evidence we have for his presence is the number of place-names, thickest in the central region and east of Scotland, which point to him or to someone of the same name. We have not a single anecdote to place alongside the delightful story of his boyhood, no record whatever of any of the many adventures which he must have had in a lifetime of pioneer missionary work. But Marnock is not alone in this. During these years of the evangelisation of our country there must have been many missionaries of whose very names we are now ignorant, or whose primitive monasteries remain only as an obscure place-name of which nothing more is known.

According to the *Aberdeen Breviary*, Marnock died and was buried at Aberchirder in the church he had founded by the River Deveron. A gruesome custom continued till the Reformation of producing the saint's skull every Sunday, washing it and giving the water to sick folk to drink—perhaps a link with Marnock's boyhood when, far away by the Shannon, the great Columba put his hand on his head.

In pre-Reformation times Marnock was regarded as patron and protector of Kilmarnock, but the only lingering, faint tradition is that he had a cell by the river bank. There is another Kilmarnock in Inverchaolan parish, Argyll. There is Dalvarnock in Glen Shira and Ardmarnock Bay on Loch Fyne. In Glasgow is Dalmarnock and in the east at Foulis-Easter he was recognised as founder and patron of the later collegiate church. At Panbride is Bothmarnock; there is a St Marny's Well in Benholm parish, Kincardineshire; and near Ballater there is a ruined church of Inchmarnock on an island in the Dee. There are Killearnans in Ross-shire and

Sutherland. His reputed burial place, Aberchir-der, had formerly the alternative title of Mar-nock.

His festival in Ireland is 18 August, but at Kilmarnock it is 25 October.

A. O. and M. O. Anderson (eds), *Adomnan's Life of Columba*, 1961

J. O'Hanlon, *Lives of the Irish Saints*, nd

MARTIN

Although in his lifetime Martin of Tours never set foot on any part of these islands, hardly any figure in this book has had a greater influence on the British Church—particularly that of north Britain.

Martin was born in Hungary just three years after toleration was granted to Christianity by the Emperor Constantine and the faith was accepted as a recognised cult. This meant that for the first time since the beginning of the faith not far short of three centuries earlier, Christians could design and erect places of worship in safety. Bishops who in previous reigns had been alternately subject to persecution or simply ignored now found themselves public figures of considerable importance and responsibility.

The great problem for the western Church during Martin's lifetime was how she should react to this new and dangerous role of playing the part of a state religion. We must conclude that she failed. One respected professor of mine, a hardened old 'voluntary' in Church politics, said loud and emphatically, 'Constantine estab-lished the Church and it has never yet reco-vered'.

Within a few years of obtaining toleration, bishops were bludgeoning each other into insen-sibility at Church councils, excommunicating each other for heresy over theological disagreements, and handing the losers over to the secular power for physical punishment and execution. In all this Martin stands not entirely blameless but at least desperately concerned and actively trying to lead the bishops into a path of understanding, piety and Christian love.

Martin was brought up as the son of a high-ranking military officer, his father being one of the few who had risen by his own capability from the ranks. Both parents were enthusiastic and devout pagans, bitterly disappointed at their son's conversion to the new faith and not a little alarmed at his attitude to his military future. Under the imperial law of the time sons of officers of certain rank had to enrol and serve the full number of years in the army. A father who had named his son after the god of war must have been disturbed at the prospect that he might be turning out to be a pacifist.

Two well-known incidents from his life illustrate ways in which he differed from his contemporaries in attitude to military service and social responsibility. When his regiment was due to proceed out against the Allemanni, Martin quietly refused to accept the usual 'donative', the sum presented to each of the soldiers before a campaign. In spite of his plea to be placed in the front of the troops without arms, 'protected not by helmet and buckskin but by the sign of the cross', he was accused of cowardice, and had his resolve really been put to the test he might have faced the ancient equivalent of a firing squad. When in the morning, however, it was found that the Germans had disappeared, the understanding commander allowed him to go free, as a civilian. If we doubt this story we must remember that his biographer, Sulpicius, had a good eye for a story worth telling, and there are some grounds for believing that Martin kept some connection with the army, perhaps as a non-combatant, for the full number of years.

A second anecdote concerns his charity. His special concern was the disabled, particularly the mentally disabled, and meeting one on a bitterly cold winter night, the young officer sliced his military cloak (capella) down the middle and gave half to the beggar. Later a little chapel was built to house the cloak and this was the origin of the word 'chapel'. The following night in a dream he heard a celestial choir singing, 'Martin, still only a catechumen, hath clothed me with this garment'.

In 361, at the age of 26, he set up his first community, on the lines of the eastern monasteries of Pachomius, in caves by the riverside at Ligugé. Here he lived as a hermit and continued doing so after he had forcibly been made bishop of Tours by the people against his will. His determination to reconcile the seclusion of the eremitic life with the duties of a Church-leader cannot have made it easy for those who had to help him with the organising of the diocese.

Ligugé had been a small community so Martin fulfilled his real hopes by moving to Marmoutier where he was soon spiritual leader of a monastery of eighty. He wrote no rules; each followed a simple ascetic life. Sulpicius embroidered his saint's life with miracles, including claims of raising from the dead, but as this was the great age of hagiography we have no way of knowing how many of these claims were believed by the writers themselves.

One of the last incidents of Martin's life was his pleading for the remission of the death sentence on the heretic Priscillian and his followers, members of a rigidly puritanical sect of Christians. This action should be seen in the context of the great Constantine himself having said that heresy must be stamped out—Martin's friend Hilary had been banished for heresy for several years and Martin himself had been subjected to a public flogging for upholding the Nicene doctrine at a time when the opposing Arians were in power. Martin himself was always against securing the victory of faith by compulsion and force and with difficulty he secured from the emperor a promise of pardon for Priscillian and his followers. He then left for his diocese and was horrified to find that when his back was turned the Priscillians had been tortured and killed. Martin was deeply affected by this, the first instance of the Church executing those with whom it was in theological disagreement. Owing to his efforts the remaining Priscillians were released.

Martin died at the age of 80 and was buried on 11 November, a day centuries later to be associated with peacemaking and reconciliation. A great shrine was erected over his remains at Tours and the cult of Martin increased until there were 4000 churches dedicated to him in France alone, and nearly 200 in Britain. During the Reformation the shrine was destroyed and the bones scattered, and during the French Revolution the site was cleared for housing. In 1860 the houses were removed and attempts made to recover the shrine. Amid the sounds of demolition the singing of the Magnificat was heard coming from the cellar; the shell of the shrine had been found bricked up beneath one of the houses.

Bede states that the see of Whithorn was dedicated to Martin but that might not refer to the original church. Martin's name occurs in conjunction with that of Ninian at many places in Britain but today many scholars believe these place-names may date only from a much later revival of interest rather than from any original connection between the two saints or their cults. At Canterbury remains of St Martin's church date back to the sixth century. At Old Brampton by Hadrian's Wall a Roman cemetery dating to the third century has within its boundaries a St Martin's church of early mediaeval date, and nearby is a St Ninian's Well. Near Dundee, Strathmartine parish has folk tales of a Christian knight fighting a dragon at Baldragon and there are other Ninian and Martin place-names nearby. The story symbolises the defeat of paganism by Martin. In other Scottish districts we find many Ninewells, which are an obvious 'Nan' or 'Ninian' derivation. A. B. Scott and other scholars of his generation took this as certain evidence of co-operation between the saints.

Martin's festival is 11 November.

E. Delamere, *St Martin*, 1963
C. Donaldson, *Martin of Tours*, 1980

mary the blessed virgin

Christians do not think of Mary as a saint in quite the same sense as the other saints in this book. Whatever our brand of Christianity, if we accept the Virgin Birth of Our Lord as a fact, Mary is unique among the saints. She alone of any created person held in her bosom the secret of the world's redemption for nine long months, then, and for the remainder of her life, knew what the profoundest theologian can only guess at—how it all happened. 'We did not make her different,' wrote Bishop Fulton Sheen, 'God did.' It is when the theologians question just how different Mary is, that the controversies which have divided the Church break out.

The Protestant accuses the Catholic, both Roman and Anglo-, of elevating the position of Mary by doctrines such as the Immaculate Conception and the Assumption and by increasing her importance in the Liturgy, until she becomes in popular devotion no longer 'the Handmaid of the Lord' but 'Regina Coeli', the Queen of Heaven. Against this the Catholic accuses the Protestant of, at the best, shameful neglect—for he may attend a church for years and never hear the Mother of Christ mentioned except for a sentence in a Christmas carol. At the worst, the Catholic sees the Protestant treatment of Mary as disrespectful.

The Catholic is more aware than most Protestants imagine of the danger that *hyperdoulia*, the special veneration which is paid to the Blessed Virgin, can too easily pass into *latreia*, the worship which must be reserved for God and Christ alone. Recently the Catholic Church has been at pains officially to emphasise that the supreme mediator must be Christ and none other. The fact that 'S' or 'St' is prefixed to Mary's name is an acknowledgement of her humanity. The prefix would never be applied to God or to Christ.

On the other hand, surely the Protestant loses a great opportunity in not employing the image of the Virgin as an example, especially to the youth of the Church. How often are girls challenged with the question, 'If God decided to be born on earth in this generation, is your body and mind such as He might choose as the vehicle?' Or how often are boys faced with the vision of a young woman of absolute purity and asked, 'How do your thoughts and your words and your life stand in her sight?' It seems a tragic legacy of the Reformation that this reticent Mother of Christ so terrifies the Protestant that he fears to include her in his prayers of thanksgiving, even at Easter when she kneels at the foot of the Cross, the sword, as had been prophesied, piercing her heart. Often, the more he proclaims his 'fundamentalism' in accepting literally the commands of scripture the less willing he is to accept that 'Henceforth all generations shall call me Blessed', or to pay heed to the Word from the Cross, 'Son, behold thy mother'.

In the period of the Celtic Church, dedication of churches to saints was not a practice; indeed, the term 'saint' had not yet been closely defined. The first dedications, which followed the mission from Northumbria of Curitan (Boniface) were to St Peter as chief of the apostles, followed by similar dedications to others of the Twelve. While there were some dedications in England, it would seem that the Virgin Mary was not generally adopted as patron in Wales until the tenth century and considerably later in Ireland, with Scotland multiplying dedications rapidly after the twelfth century.

In some cases the name of a local saint was supplanted by the Virgin or by one of the apostles, while in others the earlier dedication to the saint was retained as co-patron (St Mary and St Serf, Culross; St Mary and St Machar, Old Aberdeen). In some cases it was the local name which was used and in practice he or she was regarded as the patron.

172

The rapid development of the monastic orders in Scotland brought a great many St Mary dedications. The Cistercian order, which had the greatest number of houses, always dedicated to the Virgin, although a subsidiary patron might be placed alongside her (St Mary and St Edward, Balmerino). Among the friars, the Carmelites in Scotland originally showed St Andrew's figure on their seal, but in 1544 he was replaced by the Virgin and Child. The order was, of course, that of St Mary of Mount Carmel. Their priory at South Queensferry now serves to house the local Scottish Episcopal congregation. There were, before the Reformation, about forty collegiate churches in Scotland, and many were dedicated to St Mary, including the famous and beautiful Lincluden, near Dumfries, which had previously been a nunnery.

It would be impossible to detail the many mediaeval parishes, both Highland and Lowland, which took the Virgin as patron. Dundee parish church has always kept the name of St Mary's and both church and city have the pot of lilies which was her regular symbol. The same applied to King's College, Aberdeen, and at St Andrews the Divinity faculty today is St Mary's College.

Mary's name was also coupled to countless small chapels, chantries, wells, etc, which in time led her to be transferred to streets, wynds, closes and secular buildings. In Edinburgh, St Mary's chapel was originally the meeting place of the Incorporation of Wrights and Masons; the name became transferred to the incorporation itself, and today it is still officially known as Mary's Chapel.

In the Highlands many of the dedications are in the form of Kilmory which leads to some confusion, as the true patron may have been

Maelrubha or some other local saint whose name in Gaelic resembled Mary. Although dedications ceased following the Reformation, the name of Mary was too deeply impressed on Scottish topography for it to disappear and it survived both in the Gaelic and English forms. In the new Roman Catholic churches which arose after the end of the penal period some form of the name of the Virgin was a favourite choice, as well as the simple St Mary's. The Catholic directory lists, among others, Our Lady of Perpetual Succour, St Mary Star of the Sea, Queen of Peace, Our Lady of the Waves, St Mary of the Angels and Our Lady of Mercy.

The title of St Mary figures in no less than twenty-eight Church of Scotland congregations today, which ranks it fourth in popularity (St Andrew comes first with sixty-six, St John has thirty-two—but these would include the Baptist as well as the Evangelist—and Holy Trinity has twenty-nine). Both the Roman Catholic and Scottish Episcopal cathedrals in Edinburgh are dedicated to the Virgin.

D. Attwater, *Penguin Dictionary of Saints*, 1965

F. L. Cross and E. A. Livingstone (eds), *Oxford Dictionary of the Christian Church*, 1974

medan was supposedly one of the co-workers with Drostan and his three, but so little is known about these early Aberdeenshire missionaries that one hesitates to set down anything definite. A very large number of place-names relating to them occur throughout the north-east and there are several instances of the name Medan linked with the pictish 'pit' or 'pet' in

forms of 'Pitmaden', 'Pitmeddan', etc. Does the same missionary appear also in Galloway, or is he being confused with other saints? In that area there are Medana, Modwenna, Kirkmaiden and Maidenkirk. It is almost impossible to discover which names apply to which saint.

Airlie parish for long possessed the Bell of St Medan, some property going with the bell. Tradition affirms that in 1850 it was sold for old iron—which suggests that the property was not worth much.

In his kalendar, Forbes lists Medan under Medina.

G. A. F. Knight, *Archaeological Light on the Early Christianising of Scotland*, 1933

michael falls into quite a different category of saint from most of those dealt with in this book. He is not, as the others are, an historical figure in the Church to whom the title of saint is given because of special sanctity; he is an angelic, supernatural being, one of the seven archangels traditionally accepted by the Jews, of whom only two—Gabriel and Michael—are mentioned in scripture.

The popular concept of 'angels' (heavenly beings in human form, usually depicted dressed in some form of armour or ethereal uniform and with wings) arose, scholars now agree, when the Jews in exile came under the influence of the new Persian religion of Zoroastrianism. This religion saw in the universe and in men's hearts a perpetual struggle between the forces of light and darkness waged by good and evil spirits—the angels and the demons. The Old Testament references to Michael come naturally, therefore, in the Book of Daniel (10: 13 and 12: 1), which deals with this period of Jewish history. The New Testament passages consist of an obscure reference in Jude (verse 9) and the great vision in Revelation (12: 7–9) where Michael defeats the devil. In this passage Michael is called 'the great prince who has charge of your people' and so he was regarded as the protector of the Jewish race. Later, Christians also accepted Michael as their champion. They thought of him as not only leading the Church to ultimate victory but seeing that the individual Christian had a safe passage through the dangers of death. He was popular at periods when the Church was fighting heresy or paganism or winning converts in her mission fields; he was significant at the Christian's death-bed; and the Tridentine mass offertory had 'signifer S. Michael repraesentet eas in lucem sanctum' ('let the Standard bearer St Michael bring their souls into the holy light').

It is up to the individual Christian as to how he interprets this angelic hierarchy—as real figures in a supernatural world or as attempts to portray vividly the fact that the Church and her people are involved in spiritual battle. Of the two named archangels, Gabriel is the figure of quiet comfort who appears to the Virgin at the Annunciation, while Michael is the heavenly knight, the warlike champion. In one version of the battle of Culdreibhne, near Sligo, where Columba and the O'Donnell clan defeated the high king of Ireland, the saint dreamed the previous night that Michael announced to him that he would win the battle but that he would have to go into exile for the rest of his life. When the battle took place the heavenly figure of the archangel was seen fighting for the O'Donnells.

A peculiarity of Michael dedications is that the churches or chapels are almost invariably set on a hill or a mound. Various explanations for this have been put forward—that as a superior saint other churches should look up to his church not down upon it, that a number were fortified churches set high for defensive reasons, or (most probable) that many early British churches were built on the elevated sites of their predecessors, the pagan forts or raths.

Michael's cult spread throughout Christendom until probably he had more commemorations than any other saint except the Blessed Virgin. In some countries, as in England, his feast (29 September) became not only a major religious festival but a legal 'quarter day'—Michaelmas.

He was popular in the Celtic Church, and once the custom developed of selecting a patron instead of just naming church sites after their founding missionaries, many churches and chapels were dedicated to him, particularly during the eleventh century. In Wales many such sites are distinguished by 'Llanfihangel' ('archangel') preceding the place-name. In Scotland they appear often as Kilmichael, or, later, Kirkmichael. At least five Scottish parishes are named after Michael and there are countless church dedications, including seven in Argyll.

In the town of Linlithgow the church is dedicated to the archangel, as was a former leper hospital, and one of the town wells had inscribed on it the motto 'St Michael is kinde to straingers'. As he was regarded as a warrior, his was a favourite dedication for military chapels, as at Stirling and Rothesay castles. The village of Crossmichael in Galloway is an ancient dedication; originally a cross stood there, and around it a fair was held at Michaelmas. At Inveresk, a very ancient site, the dedication is to St Michael and All Angels—a form in which it is often found. Other pre-Reformation commemorations to the archangel include Dumfries, Dallas (Elgin), South Queensferry, Mauchline (where there is still St Michael's Well), Sprouston (in the Borders) and Dailly (Ayrshire).

F. L. Cross and E. A. Livingstone (eds), *Oxford Dictionary of the Christian Church*, 1974

MIRREN

Any allegiance or homage which the people of Paisley felt towards their saintly patron has, in these more secular days, been transferred to their football team, which bears the saint's name. Mirren, or Merinus, was one of the band of Gaidhealic missionaries trained under the great Comgall at the Irish Bangor. We are forced to depend on the later hagiographers for the few biographical details we can disentangle from the usual mass of miracles.

Mirren seems to have crossed to Britain early in his ministry; the place-name in Cornwall, Wirran or St Mirryn, is closely associated with King Constantine, and the inference has been drawn that the two missionaries continued to work together in Scotland. While Mirren's name can with some confidence be associated with Paisley and the surrounding area, the neighbouring burgh of Govan has always claimed to possess the physical remains of Constantine himself. Surrounding this there are, naturally, some doubts and difficulties—the supposed sepulchre is ornamented with figures of a much later date, and moreover, the identity of this Constantine is by no means established.

As usual the monkish historians have supplied Mirren with a royal pedigree. Probably with more truth they have made him prior of the great monastery of Bangor.

Paisley had a St Mirren's Wynd, Square, Mill and Burn. In Ayrshire, Coylton has a Knock Murren and in the Stewartry is Kirkmirren with an ancient chapel. Loch Lomond has a large island called Inchmurrin, and in the north are other, more doubtful, place-names. None could safely be used as evidence for the presence of the saint unless supported by evidence of very early usage. Forbes, pointing out that only three of the old Celtic religious houses became Clunaic monasteries (Crossraguel, Iona and Paisley), adds that the fact 'that a colony of Bangor should come to Paisley is not at all improbable'.

Mirren died around the end of the sixth century. His festival is 15 September.

A. P. Forbes, *Kalendars of Scottish Saints*, 1872
G. A. F. Knight, *Archaeological Light on the early Christianising of Scotland*, 1933

mochaoi This very early Celtic missionary is seldom honoured or remembered in Scotland, perhaps because he has been closely connected with the traditions of St Patrick, who was impressed by him as a youth and presented him with a copy of the gospels and a crozier of miraculous properties which long survived and was known as the flying, or winged, crook. The young Mochaoi followed Patrick and set up his own community at Nendruim or Nendrum, then a small island, now joined to the long, narrow Strangford Lough by a narrow causeway. The

year of Mochaoi's death at 496 is reasonably well authenticated so Nendrum is among the very early Celtic foundations, many of them probably set up by Patrick himself, and all of them considering themselves part of his 'family' ('parouchia Patricii'). Later they were often over-shadowed by the better-organised, more up-to-date Columban foundations, and this happened to Nendrum, with just a few miles to the north Magh Bhile, and nearby the even greater Beann-chor.

We cannot emphasise too often that to speak or write about Patrick's or Mochaoi's missionary work across the North Channel as 'Irish' while Ninian and the Whithorn mission is thought of as 'Scottish' gives a completely false picture of the Church of those times. The sea was not then a dividing but a unifying factor and they thought of themselves simply as two parts of a Solway Christian Church and community. Missionaries seldom confined themselves to one area but regarded it as part of their commitment to go a-wandering for Christ.

Perhaps it was this urge which drew Mochaoi over to Scotland where, in the parish of Kirk-mahoe, near Dumfries, his name is remembered, and we believe this to be the case also at Clashmahew, in the Rinns, less than a score of miles over the channel from Nendrum. Frank Knight would have us accept several other sites in south Scotland as pertaining to Mochaoi—the most probable is Kilmahoe, in Kintyre—but all are too doubtful for us to include in any list.

We do know, however, quite a lot about the Nendrum monastery, although probably much dates rather from the time of Mochaoi's immedi-ate successors. When the building which had obviously been the school was excavated some sixty years ago, dozens of metal 'scrivers', partly used slates with geometric figures and animal drawings, and other school effects were found. In Belfast museum may be seen a pupil's drawing of a horse with its back bent round to its mouth—a clever pupil's way of avoiding trouble when he had left too little room for the rest of the animal's body. Outlines of the church and the school buildings were easily identified, with metal hinges and fragments of oaken doors still in place. The stump of a great round tower close by showed signs of burning, vividly recalling the entry in the annals in the year the Vikings came: 'Sedna O'Deman, abbot of Nendrum, was burned in his own house'. Excavation of a mound of bones near the tower revealed broken heads and bones. These were of smallish round-headed men, monks sheltering from the attackers. In the end they were slaughtered as they jumped. Near the top of the mound were a few larger, long-shaped skulls, some cleft almost in two, as apparently some monks revenged themselves as they fell.

There is an interesting, unbroken succession from Patrick who gave his crozier to Mochaoi who founded Nendrum, to Caylan who was Mochaoi's successor, who taught the pupil Finian (or Finbar) who in turn founded Magh Bhile and taught the great Columba. There is often confusion between our Mochaoi and Machutus or St Malo who is wrongly given credit for the patronage of Wigtown.

Mochaoi died in 496, and his festival is 23 June.

H. C. Lawlor, *The Monastery of St Mochaoi*, 1925

E. S. Towill, 'St Mochaoi and Nendrum' in *Ulster Journal of Archaeology*, 1964

modan The seemingly simple name of

Modan is easily confused with several others. If the first syllable is no true part of the name but the very common honorific 'mo', the real word could be Mo-Aidan. Whatever the name, though, the figure seems real enough or at least as real as most of our Celtic saints can be at this distance of time.

Modan was a sixth- or seventh-century Highland Gaidheal, said to have been in his own right Laird of Benderloch. He is said to have worked intensively around the shores of the beautiful Loch Etive. Forbes gives an appreciative account of virtues attributed to the saint: 'he restricted himself to a diet of little more than bread and water. He so tamed the external senses of sight and hearing, which have been termed "the windows of death", that he never experienced the irregular motions to sin.' He founded the community of the Eglais Breac or Spotted (or Faw) Kirk (i.e. Falkirk) where today he is specially honoured. Later, he retired to the lower Clyde and spent his last years at Rosneath which regards him in a special sense as patron. Kilmodan (Glendaruel) and Balmahaodhan (Ardchattan) also remember Modan.

Many authorities make him a friend and contemporary of Ronan. Scott puts his death in the eighth century but Farmer puts it almost two centuries earlier. Sometimes he is confused with an abbot of north Scotland of the same name.

His festival is 4 February.

A. P. Forbes, *Kalendars of Scottish Saints*, 1872
A. B. Scott, *The Pictish Nation*, 1918

modwenna and
triduana

Myths, legends and traditions surrounding these two female missionaries centre on different districts of Scotland—Modwenna in Galloway, Triduana in Edinburgh and the Highlands—but they both incorporate such closely related versions of what may be called 'the thorn myth' that they are best treated in a single note.

Modwenna (also called Medina, Monenna and Edana) had held the rank of princess in Ireland (as we expect in such cases). After conversion to Christianity by none other than St Patrick, she crossed to Galloway to avoid the amorous advances of a lover. With two handmaids, she dwelt in a cave at Portankill where she built a small chapel near where the hamlet of Maiden-kirk was later to arise. Unfortunately her Irish lover had followed her. The story is best continued from that point by C. H. Dick, who clothed the brief outline of the legend with drama and literary power:

> Her soldier rushed in and threw his arms about her. She slipped from his grasp and, followed by her handmaids, rushed into the surf and took refuge on a rock amid the water. Her lover hasted after her, but before he could reach her the rock floated off and carried its precious burden across to Monreith Bay, where Medina found a short-lived peace. The lover found her new place of retreat. When he came into sight the lady promptly climbed a tree. 'Why persecute me thus?' she exclaimed. 'Those eyes compel me,' her lover began, but before he could say more she tore them out and threw them at his feet, crying 'Take them then!'

At this, her lover departed, broken-hearted. The saint climbed down and asked her maids for water to wash her bleeding face, but unfortunately they did not have any. Immediately a clear spring burst forth from the rocks. The story ends with her sight being restored. Later the chapel in her honour was built at Kirkmaiden-in-Fernis, near Monreith House, whose owner, Sir Herbert Maxwell, it is said, used to tell the story and point out the very rock the saint had sailed on and the well where she bathed her eyes.

In this version of the legend the thorns do not actually enter, but there is the significant plucking out of the eyes to achieve disfiguration and secure chastity. In addition another popular Celtic legend is introduced in the shape of the rock which floats and serves the purpose of a boat. Sometimes it is an altar on which the saint floats, sometimes a rock, but the tale is linked with several Celtic saints.

In the Triduana setting of what is obviously the same legend, the heroine is supposed to have arrived in Scotland with the party which St Curitan (or Boniface) brought to Invergowrie. She set up a small community with a chapel at Rescobie in Angus. At this point her pursuing lover enters the story and to our surprise turns out to be none other than Nechtan the saint—the king whom we have already met in the story of Curitan. He did later give up his throne and become a monk. Perhaps the story has just that amount of truth that he had truly desired the young nun for his wife, and his fruitless attempts to win her led to the magnification which coupled a true if unfortunate love story with a popular legend.

As we suspected she would, Triduana sought refuge from him. Fleeing to the Celtic settlement of Dunfallandy in Perthshire she was again pursued; this time it was a thorn tree the maid climbed, obviously to render pursuit more painful. Nechtan, however, climbed after her, so she plucked out both her eyes and, skewering them on two thorn bushes, flung them down to him. The very words used before this action are almost the same as in Modwenna's case: 'What does so great a prince desire of a poor virgin dedicated to God?' which receives the reply, 'The most excellent beauty of thine eyes.'

In this version there is no word of her getting back her sight. After various missionary journeys in the north she retires to Restalrig between Leith and Edinburgh where she remains till her death, caring for a holy well whose waters acquire fame as a cure for diseases of the eyes. (This is probably the same lady who, as Moyanne, is associated at Burton-on-Trent with a similar legend of uninvited love.)

As Medina the first of these saints is remembered in the ruins of the landing place at Portankill where there is also St Medan's cave, and across Luce Bay there is a St Medana's Well at Monreith. She is also linked with Dundonald Hill in Ayrshire where she had a chapel. She is supposed to have brought five virgins to Edinburgh who may have given the castle its title of Castrum Puellarum. On Traprain Law her chapel was linked with the story of Enoch. Her seventh and last chapel was on the site of the present Invergowrie church. She was also said to have several monasteries in England.

The old kirk at Restalrig is specially linked with Triduana; the well, though oily and muddy is still thought to be a cure for sore eyes. The Reformers so deprecated the many pilgrimages to Restalrig that the church was the object of their first attacks in the area.

In the *Orkneyinga Saga* she appears as Trollhoena who miraculously cured Bishop John of Caithness after he had had his eyes blinded and his tongue cut out. In Papa Westray she appears as St Tredwell. Kinellar (Aberdeenshire) is in her patronage and her connection with Dunfallandy has been mentioned.

Her festival is 8 October or 9 November.

C. H. Dick, *Highways and Byways in Galloway and Carrick*, 1915

D. H. Farmer, *Oxford Dictionary of Saints*, 1978

J. Grant, *Old and New Edinburgh*, 1883

MOLIOS As in so many other cases the honorific prefix 'mo' tends to obscure the true name of this saint. He is connected with Arran, particularly with Lamlash (which is derived from his name) and with Holy Island (Arran) where he probably had his desertum and where some outstanding rock carvings may indicate his presence. He must be distinguished from the missionary of the same name who dwelt on the small island of Devenish in Lough Erne who was said to be 'anamchara' (soul-friend) to Columcille. Our Molios (or Laisren or Molaise) was of the royal Ulster line and is said to have refused the kingship of the province. On his mother's side he was the grandson of Aedan mac Gabran, king of Dalriada.

Molios's early training was probably at Kingarth, as St Blane was his uncle. After returning to Ireland for a time, he came back to Scotland to avoid the honour of the Ulster throne, and he made his missionary centre on the small Holy Island off Lamlash. In the controversy over the date of Easter he took the Roman side, against his old tutor, Fintan Munnu. Near Port-Bannatyne he is probably remembered in Ardmaleish, and up Loch Fyne at Kilmaglas, which a Strachur Charter refers to as 'Capella

Sancti Malachi' for 'Molaise'. In Ireland he was reckoned founder of the large monastery of Inishmurray and was thought to be abbot of Old Leighlin. Today in Ireland his cult centres on Inishmurray.

Tradition asserted that he returned to his favourite Holy Island where he died, after voluntarily accepting thirty diseases in expiation for his sins.

His festival is 18 April.

D. H. Farmer, *Oxford Dictionary of Saints*, 1978
A. P. Forbes, *Kalendars of Scottish Saints*, 1872
G. A. F. Knight, *Archaeological Light on the Early Christianising of Scotland*, 1933

moluag This saint's proper name was Lugaidn, pronounced Lua, which, with the honorific 'mo' prefixed, gives the usual form of the name. Other forms are Lugadh, Luanus, Moloack and even Mulvey and Simmerluak.

Moluag was founder and leader of the missionary community on the island of Lismore off the Appin shore and has been variously described as fierce rival or friendly colleague to Columba of Iona. He had been trained at the Irish Bangor by Comgall and is mentioned in St Bernard's *Life of Malachy* as one of the sons of Comgall's holy community who are each reported to have founded one hundred monasteries.

It has been suggested that Moluag and Columba were rivals as they were of different racial stock—Columba an Irish Gaidheal, Moluag an Irish Pict or Cruithne. Few today would accept that 'Pict' has much relevance to racial or tribal divisions in Ireland, but the Cruithni were probably of stock distinct from Gaidheals although by Moluag's day speaking Gaelic and losing their distinctive traits. Many of these Irish missionaries attached themselves to Pictish areas when they came to Scotland. Dedications today suggest that Moluag evangelised in the north-west mainland and northern isles, from Lismore, while from Iona Columba worked among the Dalriada incomers.

The traditional story of the rivalry is that both missionaries wanted Lismore as their headquarters and raced for the island in coracles. Moluag, in danger of losing, sliced off his thumb and threw it ashore to stake his claim, crying, 'My flesh and blood have first possession of the island and I bless it in the name of the Lord'. Columba, in temper, cursed it: 'The rocks will grow edge uppermost' and 'May you have only alder for your fuel!' To this burst of temper Moluag mildly replied, 'But the rocks will not hurt to walk upon and the alder will burn like tinder.' It is said today that the upended strata makes easy walking and the alder kindles well.

Columba might be excused for his temper, for Lismore was probably a more suitable centre than Iona, at least for evangelising the mainland. Later it was not the more famous Iona but Lismore which became the cathedral seat of the bishopric of the Isles. Columba is said to have jeered at the small 'rath' surrounding the monastery, but from it went its leader and his monks to found churches throughout the west Highlands. They went into Inverness-shire and to the Black Isle, where Moluag made a second centre at Rosemarkie, and then into Banffshire where Mortlach, along with Clatt, became a lesser focal point for work in the Aberdeenshire uplands.

Tradition states that it was at Rosemarkie that the saint died in 592, near the spot where later the Pictish Church erected a great slab of rose-pink stone with the Christian cross amid the traditional Pictish emblems from its pagan days. In the thirteenth century the church of St Moluag at Lismore was made the cathedral of the bishopric of the isles. The parish church today incorporates part of the chancel.

Moluag's blackthorn staff or crook (the Bachail Mor or Bachail Buidhe) has very fortunately been preserved. Traditionally in the keeping of the Livingstone family, the Barons of Bachail, it was for long the property of the Dukes of Argyll. In 1814 an ancient iron bell was discovered at Kilmichael Glassary which was believed to come from Lismore. It is now in the Museum of Antiquities in Edinburgh.

In the Isles, variant forms of Kilmaluag are found at Kilmuir (Skye), Treshnish Point (Mull), Tiree, Raasay, Pabbay, etc. In Kintyre we find Killdaloig (da is an ancient form for mo), and there are links with the saint at Renfrew, Alyth (St Malogue's Fair), Cromdale and Inverfarigaig (Loch Ness). He is patron of Mortlach (Banffshire) and in Aberdeenshire variations of the name are found at Clatt and at Clova. Moluag's name is found, indeed, in almost every Highland parish.

His festival is 4 August.

D. Pochin Mould, *The Irish Saints,* 1964
W. D. Simpson, *The Celtic Church in Scotland,* 1935

monan is a most difficult saint to identify. The Fife fishing community which takes this name is often wrongly written St Monance, but of course should be St Monans. But this begs the real question: was the 'mo' part of his name, or was it the common prefix meaning 'my dear'?

In this case the saint would be 'Mo . . .', i.e. Monenn, Monenna, or even Ninian. Indeed, in some lists of Irish saints, Monenn of Cloncurry is taken as another name for Ninian.

An elaborate and impossible story in the mediaeval *Aberdeen Breviary* states that Monan came from Hungary to preach in Fife but was murdered on May Island. With his usual confidence, Frank Knight identifies Monan with Moinend, the companion of Brendan of Clonfert. The whole life is so doubtful that one cannot with any confidence set any dates.

A. B. Scott, *The Pictish Nation*, 1918

MONIRUS The crowds which throng Crathie during royal visits think little and care less about that church's own saint. Little is known about the rather late missionary, Monirus (also called Manire or Niniar), whose death date is 824, if the traditions are reliable. His work was in the Dee valley in Aberdeenshire and around Balvenie in Banff. The pagan natives of Auchendryne attempted to murder him and he fled to the hill of Cairn Na Moine where he collapsed but was miraculously revived on drinking from a spring which flowed from the hill. It seems strange that he should have met such opposition if tradition be correct that missionaries had evangelised the area long before Monirus came. Returning to Auchendryne he founded a 'muinn-tir'. He had some success later at Crathie for in addition to a church in his name he was remembered by an annual fair. A pool in the Dee is still called Polmanuire.

Monirus's contests with local pagans resemble St Patrick's contests with the druids. When he was being refreshed by spring water, it dried up in answer to a pagan priest's prayer but flowed again when the missionary blessed it in the name of the Virgin.

Monirus died in 824 and his festival is 18 December.

Hathalan was an Aberdeenshire saint of some interest, for behind the biography there appears to be the picture of one who, before his time, practised natural cultivation of the land, precursor of those today who employ hygrometry and natural aids to produce their crops. Appropriately, when other crops in his district failed and people faced starvation Nathalan's were producing abundantly. But, in another season, when his crops showed signs of failure he lost faith and blamed God. Ashamed of himself, he bound his right arm to his side and vowed not to unlock the key until he had made pilgrimage to the shrines of both Peter and Paul. To make his task more difficult, apparently, he had meantime thrown the key into the River Dee. Visiting Rome and seeing on every side the monuments of the saints, he bewailed his sin, and adored the Creator whom he had offended. He then met a boy who was selling a little fish which Nathalan purchased. In its belly he found the key, unrusted, which he had flung into the River Dee. As a result, so the mediaeval narrative continues, the Supreme Pontiff made him a bishop.

At his own expense Nathalan founded churches at Tullich, Bothelnie (Old Meldrum) and Coull, and on his death in 678 it is said that the body was carried from Bothelnie to Tullich where he had spent his boyhood.

His festival is 8 January.

G. A. F. Knight, *Archaeological Light on the Early Christianising of Scotland*, 1933

nicholas Stories of the life of Nicholas of Myra in Asia Minor, although verging on the legendary and unsupported by historical evidence, show him to have been among the most interesting and colourful of saints. He was appointed bishop probably during the persecution of the emperor Diocletian while still very young because the more notable and mature Christians had either been executed or forced into hiding. To avoid arrest he became adept at disguising his person and the familiar beard of Santa Claus is an adaptation of one of his disguises. Appropriately, he is considered the patron saint of all detectives. He is also patron of architects, for during his bishopric he made plans to build a splendid cathedral for the days when persecution was ended; it was said he constructed a working model of the project, which entitles him to be considered the patron saint of model-makers.

Another means he employed to avoid arrest was to work his passage round the Mediterranean, and in so doing he became a capable sailor. He has always been a popular saint with seafaring communities and in our country there are many ancient dedications to him in the Orkney Isles and in our coastal towns. Although his episcopate was somewhat unconventional, in doctrine he was extremely orthodox. He is supposed (but without historical probability) to have attended the great Nicaean council in 325 and when he heard the heretic Arius speaking he rose and hit him squarely on the jaw. Perhaps for this he might be considered patron of all boxers and boxing matches.

He is particularly noted for his kindness to children and many legends have gathered round his name for such deeds. On one occasion when he heard that three young women could not marry because their father was unable to afford the dowries, Nicholas crept onto the roof of their house during the night and dropped three gold pieces down the chimney for them. Now the coins are symbolised in the pawnbroker's three gold balls, and members of that trade have always considered Nicholas their patron.

A legend sometimes represented in the stained-glass of Nicholas churches shows how a wicked inn-keeper kidnapped three small boys, murdered them and salted their bodies in barrels in his cellar ready to be served to his guests when sufficiently matured. When Bishop Nicholas heard of this grisly deed he crept into the cellar by night, located the barrels and by making the sign of the cross over them restored the boys to life.

By a roundabout route Nicholas has become our Santa Claus, for his figure, originally dressed as a mediaeval bishop, was taken from Holland to New Amsterdam by Dutch settlers, transferred to the English immigrants when the town became New York, and eventually brought back to us in the very different attire we see him in at our parties. The saint's festival is 6 December, and it is on this day that most European children receive their gifts, but in Britain the occasion has been merged with the Christmas celebration on 25 December. Much revered throughout the eastern Churches, Nicholas is patron saint of Russia. He has also been patron of Aberdeen since early in the Middle Ages; her great church, later divided, was named for him, and there were several local ceremonies connected with the saint. It is said that on the festival each year the grammar school rector took one of his pupils round collecting funds, attired as a bishop. When James VI sailed to Denmark to collect his bride the city provided a vessel named *Nicholas* for the squadron.

He is remembered by a parish on Stronsay, a chapel at Shapinsay and one in St Magnus cathedral. Leith, as we would expect from a busy sea-port, was especially partial to Nicholas, with a chapel and a hospital. Both played a prominent part in the town's history until General Monk cleared the ground for his defences. Until recent unions the Church of Scotland had a congregation of this name among her Leith churches. Other sea-ports like Dundee, Crail, Ayr, and St Andrews honoured him with chapels. Formerly, Uphall and Dalkeith were dedicated to him. The modern extension charge of St Nicholas, Sighthill, Edinburgh was so named because it was funded with contributions from Sunday schools.

J. D. Douglas, *New International Dictionary of the Christian Church*, 1974

J. M. Mackinlay, *Ancient Church Dedications in Scotland*, Vol 2, 1914

ΠΙΠΙΩΠ Had Ninian appeared from the pages of history as more substantial, he would surely have competed against Columba or Kentigern for the honour of patron of Scotland, and put up a strong case against the outsider, Andrew, who had only his apostolic title and eye-witness position to commend him. None of the early saints is without perplexing problems which are left for historians to resolve, and although it has rightly been claimed that we know twice as much about Ninian as was known twenty years ago, knowledge of him does seem to progress in cycles.

In the nineteenth century he was generally regarded as a kindly father figure to the Scottish Church. This was actually little more than folk-myth or legend; he had converted some fierce Picts, but had not St Patrick told us of their ultimate apostasy? During the early part of this century, however, the saint of Whithorn found a champion who took him very seriously indeed. Dr Archibald Scott seemed convinced that all good features in the Scottish Church were ultimately traceable to Candida Casa and the race called Picts. Columba and his Gaidealic missionaries, who had hitherto had it all their own way, now found many hitherto accepted theories not only challenged but despised. Scott, whose patriotism seemed often to influence his scholarship, linked Columba and all Gaidheals with the anti-British Irish rebels—so all true Scotsmen must be radically Britons or Picts. I trust these words do not wrong the late Dr Scott, but repeated perusal of his *Pictish Nation* and his *Rise and Relations of the Church of Scotland* reinforce this view, and it is noticeable that he is absent from any references in almost all modern works on the Celtic Church.

In his day Scott found modified support for his views from G. A. F. Knight who published two impressive volumes detailing the lives and supposed journeys of hundreds of missionary 'saints' of the Celtic period. Knight's work involved much invaluable labour, but he accepted the slightest of evidence far too uncritically and treated every church dedication as if it were proof positive of a personal foundation.

W. Douglas Simpson's contribution to this pro-Pictish movement was to relate the Christianising of north Britain to the map of Roman penetration. In the end Simpson found himself acting as rearguard to the claims for Ninianic sites which had been taken to reach up to the far north and even to the Shetlands. The majority of these sites Simpson discarded until he was left with only three or four.

During the controversy one scholar remained largely unimpressed by the extravagant claims for a conversion of most of Scotland from Candida Casa. In his book *The Columban Church*, J. A. Duke re-emphasised the work of Columba and the influence of Iona.

Since the days of Scott and his followers (all of whom were considerable scholars) a new generation of specialists has arisen with fresh contributions to make. Amongst these, the name of Charles Thomas stands out. For the first time he, and others with him, have sought the help of field archaeology to solve some of the problems of Celtic church sites. His Iona excavation has already forced us to amend our views on the position of the muinntir and of what went on within it. Applecross is another example of the same and above all Thomas's Isles of Fleet dig at Ardwall has revealed that within a few years many of our ideas about these early missionaries may need radical revision.

One subject which has been engaging the attention of those interested in the early British Church has concerned the nature of Church government. Within the first three centuries a fairly uniform hierarchical system arose: bishop—priest—deacon. This was based originally on the Roman civil government which was centred on towns or cities with their surrounding districts, which became 'dioceses'. The late Canon Streeter, however, showed that in many remote areas this three-fold tier of clergy was not practicable and a number of clerics sharing equal responsibility emerged, sometimes with one more experienced 'bishop' in charge.

During the fifth and sixth centuries in Britain, Ireland and perhaps also elsewhere, a strangely different form of government became universal in the local Churches. This was based not on bishoprics (dioceses) but on the many large monasteries which had become the centres from which the faith spread and which housed the clergy. Such communities possessed bishops, often a large number of them, but while they (and only they) had certain powers (such as ordination), the government of the monastery was firmly under the control of the 'abbot', a position which tended to become hereditary (as was the case with Iona). No one today can doubt that this was the form of the British and Irish Churches until after the synod of Whitby when the Celtic Churches gradually and often reluctantly conformed to the Roman practice, and the diocesan bishop with monarchical powers was introduced. The problem, essentially, is this: was the process simply the reintroduction of a form which had existed originally in the Church in Ninian's day before the rise of monasticism, or was it introduced for the first time? The fashion today is to suggest that the British Church was originally governed by bishops and was diocesan. It has been suggested that these bishoprics corresponded territorially with the old kingdoms into which the land had been divided—Kentigern, according to this theory, would be bishop of Strathclyde, and Ninian probably of Whithorn, a minor see depending on the more important Carlisle.

The theory is attractive, but, I fear, far from the true picture. It is difficult to envisage the British Church of the fourth or fifth centuries as being anything like efficient enough in organisation for such a picture to have much meaning. Of course it is possible to imagine bishops—were not the remains of some dug up at Whithorn?—but they were probably chorepiscopoi, episcopoi vagantes, country bishops moving from place to place and seeing their office as very little different from the rest of the clerical missionaries, who were presbyters. Some recent Roman Catholic theologians have been stressing that the step from presbyter to bishop in earlier times was a less significant one than that between layman and cleric. I feel sure that in St Patrick's life the emphasis shown in the early biographies was on 'ordination' and the further step of 'consecration' (as it was beginning to be called) did not imply anything as important as the step from presbyter to bishop does today. Of course, the early British Church was not monastic (under Patrick, Ninian or anyone else), and had a simple version of the three orders, but within that framework distinctions were not well defined until the Church had passed through the monastic phase under the Celtic abbots. There is no question but that Columba always remained a presbyter, and in the case of Patrick the step between presbyter and bishop is scarcely noted in the biographies. Too often the bishop figure behind the writings of some modern scholars is suspiciously near that of the modern diocesan, monarchical bishop.

From discussion of the type of government in the early British Church, we turn to some consideration of Ninian himself and the set-up at Candida Casa. Although Ninian is almost a contemporary of Patrick we have for him nothing like the material we have for the Ulster saint, although probably they were born within a few miles of each other, if not at the same place. The

Confessio and the *Epistola* are generally accepted as Patrick's own works. There is also some miscellaneous material and, within two centuries of his death two biographies, by Muirchu and Tirechan. For Ninian, on the other hand, literary evidence begins in the eighth century with a paragraph in Bede's *History*, part of which, he tells us, was gathered from general gossip. Until recently the only other authority was the twelfth century *Life* by the monk Ailred, which is more concerned with the miraculous than the historical. Recently two ancient poems have been edited and these appear to be contemporary with Bede and of great importance for the study of our saint.

The *Miracula Nynie Episcopi* is important for what it does not say. There is no mention of a visit to Martin or a dedication to him, the Rome visit is placed differently, nor is Ninian of noble birth. The visit to Martin has for long been used to claim a close connection between Scottish Church traditions and those of Gaul. This must now be based on other evidence, as the *Miracula* would surely have noted such a visit had it taken place.

Bede's passage on Ninian, which some think was added later to his history, is well known and need not be repeated. Its gist is that, a long time before St Columba, the southern Picts had accepted the true faith through the preaching of Bishop Ninian, who had been regularly instructed at Rome. He goes on to say that Ninian's own episcopal see is named after St Martin, is famous for its stately church and is in the English province of Bernicia (Northumbria).

It needs close examination of this passage, which at first looks so simple, to note the difficulties and doubts it raises.

First, it is now accepted that there were no Picts in Galloway: 'southern Picts' were those in modern Angus and the Mearns. Why then did Ninian, himself a Briton with his see at Whithorn, go to a different nation at a considerable distance to find a field to evangelise? If being a bishop at that date implies having a diocese, what was he doing so far from its centre?

Second, was the name of Martin attached to Whithorn in the time of Ninian? Celtic missionaries did not dedicate their churches but usually named them after their founders. Could this dedication have come much later after Anglian influence re-established Whithorn as a bishopric?

What was the saint's real name? We only have Latinised versions, and know the Brythonic only in an ablative form.

Stones in the district undoubtedly point to very early Christian culture but so far nothing has been found linking 'Ninian' with the site.

Although many Scottish place-names have a Ninianic connection (St Ninian's, St Ringan's, St Trinnean's etc), they are all from later language roots and may only date from some centuries later when Ninian's cult had become popular, or when the Church was playing up Ninian against the popular cult of Columba.

Was Ninian really a pioneer? The tendency lately has been to treat him not as the pioneer of Christianity in Galloway but as establishing the bishopric for the area. Thomas has argued for this and points to sites suggesting similar dioceses for Lothian, Tweeddale and Strathclyde.

Physical remains at Whithorn today will disappoint the visitor. The various early crosses and stones are carefully cared for, otherwise there are only portions of the much later mediaeval church which in its day witnessed so many pilgrimages. Interesting coffins of early bishops recently uncovered are not on view, nor is there any sign of the white plaster which led many to assert that at last we would see the real Candida Casa.

The district around Whithorn will probably provide more of interest and excitement than Whithorn itself. Four miles to the south at the tip of the peninsula is the delightful little village of the Isle of Whithorn. Here there is a neat but roofless mediaeval chapel which, formerly, some scholars believed might be the original Ninianic monastery. When Charles Thomas excavated, however, no Celtic period remains were found, although in the days of pilgrimages thousands must have made their last halt here before reaching Whithorn and qualifying for one of the medallions with which pilgrims were rewarded when they completed their task.

Westward along the coast a leafy farm road leads to a pebbled beach where a large cave marks the 'desertum' or retreat of some early saint, both by constant tradition and by location, probably of Ninian himself. This is Physgill. The crosses picked out on the walls have been left for us to see but most of the marked stones have been moved for safety to Whithorn. From time to time the cave floor has been cleared so that it cannot now look very like the cave of the saint's day.

On our way back through the peninsula it is well worth taking the side road which goes by Kirkmadrine where, set into the wall of a disused kirk, is a group of three stones, among the most ancient Christian stones in the country. Once used as farm gate-posts they are now well protected and they show the 'labarum' or sign of the cross which Constantine saw in the sky before his decisive battle. Their probable date is a little later than Ninian, but in Whithorn museum is the Latinus stone, dated about the time of the saint himself.

At another site in the Stewartry, on Ardwall, one of the little Isles of Fleet, Charles Thomas has revealed no less than three distinct layers of Celtic church remains. These show the development which took place from the earliest days until the end of that period of history. At the top and latest level was a remarkably clean cut slab with an inscription to one Cudgar, a cleric obviously of importance, probably in the Anglian period. This site and others which may be unearthed nearby may play an important part in future study of Candida Casa.

There is scarcely a parish in Scotland which does not possess, through place-names or otherwise, some memorial to St Ninian. All, however, are in later forms of the name, altered as the language of the people changed. We know now that Scott and his followers were too credulous when they accepted these as signs of Ninian's presence, or as contemporary with him. It is now recognised as more probable that they represent traces of a very active Ninian cultus dating from the twelfth or even the eighth century. Finally, identification of Ninian with the saint Moninne, often attempted, is very unlikely.

Ninian's festival is 16 September.

J. Macqueen, *St Nynia*, 1961
C. Thomas, *Christianity in Roman Britain*, 1981
C. Thomas, *The Early Christian Archaeology of North Britain*, 1972

OJohn Ogilvie

The first papal canonisation creating saints did not take place until the Church had been in existence for twelve centuries. Among early saints was Scotland's Queen Margaret in 1250. In the eighth century Adamnan and his companions were recognised, but without formal processes of canonisation. There have been no further canonisations affecting Scotland until 1976, when the final processes for the canonisation of John Ogilvie were completed. He is the only post-Reformation figure to find a place in these pages.

Ogilvie came of the cadet branch of a family well known in north-east Scotland. He was born in Banffshire so it is hardly correct to call him, as some books do, a Highlander, for most people from this corner of the country reject the title. They are of different stock and have a distinctly different accent.

It was this part—Moray, Nairn, Banff and Aberdeen—which at the Reformation clung most closely to 'the Old Faith', and districts like the Enzie and the Cabrach nurtured a new generation of priests. This mission of the Counter-Reformation, as we might expect, became the especial care of the Society of Jesus, or Jesuits. It was the Jesuits who in the end trained and ordained the new saint, but by a roundabout route, for, while surrounded by the Catholicism of the district, his father, and as far as we know his other relatives, were Calvinists and emphatically Protestant.

In 1592 at the age of 13 the lad left home to complete his education on the continent—quite usual in those days for one in his station in society. At some point during the four years of his travels he turned from Calvinism to Catholicism. His personal arguments for this step were simple. The Protestants, he felt, lacked unity, antiquity and the power of miracles. In 1596 he applied for admission to the Scots college of Douai, then housed at Louvain. Its students were largely from Scottish noble families. Within two years he was transferred to the Benedictine college at Ratisbon, then back to the Jesuits at Olmutz. He became a novice in 1599.

His desire after his ordination was to return to the Jesuit mission in Scotland, and he knew only too well the dangerous nature of such work. Not until 1613 did his superiors allow him to join the Scottish mission. At the time Scots Catholicism was at a low ebb; James had allowed the consecration of Episcopalian bishops but intensified his persecution of the Catholics. Ogilvie, because of the penal laws, travelled as a horse-dealer or a soldier. For a short period he removed to London but was sharply instructed by the authorities to return to Scotland where he found friendship and relative safety for a time with William Sinclair and his Catholic household. He ministered for a time in Glasgow and Renfrew as well as Edinburgh and his arrest came unexpectedly in Glasgow market-place where he was betrayed as a priest by one Adam Boyd, a nephew of the sheriff, who introduced himself as wanting instruction in the Catholic faith. Ogilvie was imprisoned both in Glasgow and in Edinburgh and during his imprisonment suffered torture, not so much physical as mental and psychological, through being deprived of sleep and propped upright for long periods (methods strangely ahead of the time for they are similar to what is employed in modern psychological torture). Only when he was certified near to death was any respite granted.

His 'examination' was largely conducted by Archbishop Spotteswood and King James himself. With his keen brain and aptitude for abstruse points of logic, the king delighted in interrogations when he could show his opponent at a disadvantage. With his usual cunning he arranged the questioning so that the indictment was not about religion but about treason. Unlike the Fawkes affair in England there was no question of a plot against James, so the questions were directed at proving that, while in a Catholic's eyes the Pope was always infallible, the king was not and that a heretic king might legitimately be deposed by the Pope. Ogilvie was offered the provostship of Moffat and the archbishop's daughter if he renounced the Pope.

The result of the examination was a foregone conclusion. The scaffold had already been prepared. At the end, Ogilvie asked the prayers of the Virgin, the Angels and the Saints. Below the scaffold the crowd of Glasgow citizens, mainly Protestants, were committing the unfortunate priest to God's mercy. 'If there be heere any hidden catholikes, let them pray for me,' came the final words from the scaffold, 'but the prayers of heretics I will not have.' On all sides it was an age of intolerance.

John Ogilvie's festival is 10 March.

C. D. Ford, *A Highlander for Heaven*, 1976

Olaf Haraldsson is remembered as the king and patron saint of Norway. In his time, he fought for England against the Danes. He faced a rebellion by Cnut, was exiled in 1029 and was killed in battle the following year. It is doubtful, some might say, whether Olaf should legitimately be included in any reputable kalendar of saints for he employed forcible and bloody means to persuade his subjects to accept Christian baptism, giving them a straightforward choice of accepting the new faith or stepping forward for execution.

After his death, however, came many reports of miracles, and the belief that his body remained uncorrupted led to the rapid growth of his cult and sanctification. In England the gruesome emblems on the graveyard gates of St Olave's, Hart Street (the parish church of Samuel Pepys) appealed to Charles Dickens. This church was badly blitzed but later beautifully restored. Both York and Exeter commemorate Olaf, or Olave, in parish churches of considerable beauty. In Scotland the surname Macaulay probably derives from Amlaibh (Aulag), Gaelic for Olaf, and there were several parishes, mostly in Orkney and Shetland, claiming his patronage. The less common Tola arose from prefixing the T of 'St' to his name.

His festival is 29 July.

D. Attwater, *Penguin Dictionary of Saints*, 1965

Oswald
The kalendar of saints includes many kings and royal personages, but few are as worthy of being named 'saint' as Oswald of the Anglo-Saxon kingdom of Northumbria.

Oswald's parentage would not suggest that he might become a saint, for his father Aethelfrith earned his nickname of 'the destroyer'. In 603 he defeated King Aedan of Dalriada at Deagsastan and moved south to meet the British, or Welsh, army in 613 at Chester. There he left Christians aghast by turning on the monks who had gathered near the battlefield to pray for victory for their Welsh compatriots. Without arms and offering no resistance, only fifty of 1200 escaped his fury. Aethelfrith in his turn fell in battle against the East Angles near Bawtry and his relative Edwin was free to return to his own country and ascend the throne.

The accession of King Edwin was something of a tragedy for Aethelfrith's family. His three sons, Eanfrid, Oswald and Oswy and his daughter had to be hurried to the safety of exile and completed their childhood far to the west in Iona where they heard the Gaelic tongue of the Scots as well as the Latin of the monks, and shared the life of laymen in the monastery. No records have been left to let us know what impressions the island made on the young refugees—Eanfrid as the eldest must surely have led them across the Machar to picnic at St Columba's Bay and in scrambles up the rocks. Surely the spouting cave would be to them as great an attraction as it is to children today. There would, however, be no Martyrs' Bay, for the Fair and Dark Gentiles from the north had not yet come in their Viking ships to kill and plunder.

Away east in Northumbria, Edwin and his people had accepted Christianity. His palace at Gefrin in the shadow of Yeavering Bell among the Cheviots (whose outlines may be traced today by aerial survey) lay beside the little River Glen, almost directly on the border of Scotland and England. In one thirty-six-day mission of St Paulinus from Canterbury, 3000 Northumbrians were dipped in the waters for Christian baptism. Tradition asserts that Edwin himself was baptised at York but it is equally possible that it was up on these moors that he received the cleansing water. Just five years later, however, in 632, Edwin himself fell in battle—the Christian king of the Saxons slain by the Christian king Cadwallon of Gwynedd.

The royal exiles were now free to return. There was a period of great confusion in which Eanfrid, the eldest son, was brutally murdered by Cadwallon in York. Oswald prepared to fight to drive back to the west the Britons and restore Northumbria to the Anglo-Saxons. He gathered his army beside the ruins of the wall the Romans had built in the Tyne valley. Cadwallon marched north. The armies came to grips at the place later called Heavenfield. After fierce fighting the British fled; Cadwallon was caught some miles away and killed. Oswald returned to his capital of Bamburgh in triumph. On the night before the battle he had seen a vision of St Columba spreading out his robe to cover not only himself but the whole army. His must be a Christian nation, he determined, and he turned for missionaries, not, as had been done before, to Canterbury, but to Iona, the place of his own exile. The account of Aidan told of the close co-operation and friendship between King Oswald and the saint who led the Iona missionaries and who established their new community on the island of Lindisfarne. Bede notes, 'It was most delightful to see the king himself interpreting the Word of God to his thanes and leaders; for he himself had obtained perfect command of the Scottish tongue during his long exile ... Although he wielded supreme power Oswald was always humble, kindly and generous

209

to the poor and strangers.' He goes on to tell of an Easter meal when, as the king was about to be served from a silver dish, he was informed by a servant that a great crowd of starving peasants were outside. The king at once ordered his own food to be taken out to them and the silver dish to be broken up and divided among them. 'Bishop Aidan,' writes Bede, 'caught hold of the royal hand and exclaimed "May this hand never perish!" When Oswald was killed in battle his hand and arm were severed from his body and remain uncorrupted to this day. They are preserved in a silver casket in the church of St Peter in the royal city which is called Bebba' (Bamburgh).

In this account of King Oswald, the usual tradition, established by Bede, is accepted that Paulinus of Canterbury conducted the first Northumbrian mission and baptised King Edwin. A quite different account in the Welsh sources ascribes it to one Rhun, son of Urien of Rheged. In this case the inference is that the first Christian assault on Northumbria came from the Britons of Cumbria (Rheged) rather than from Canterbury.

The site of Heavenfield may be easily recognised a mile south of Chollerford. It has a replica of the great wooden cross which was erected after the battle and in a field nearby is little St Oswald's church, kept clean and seemly for the occasional services still held there. There are not many commemorations to Oswald in Scotland whereas in England over sixty parishes honour him. We have Kirkoswald in Ayrshire with a corresponding parish across the Solway in Cumbria. Cathcart had him as patron in olden days, Carluke had both a church and chapel to Oswald and in the east Whittingehame was traditionally his.

Oswald died in 642, and his festival is 28 February.

R. Anderson, *The Violent Kingdom*, 1971

P. Hunter Blair, *Roman Britain and Early England*, 1963

B. Colgrave and R. A. B. Mynors (eds), *Bede: Historia Ecclesiastica*, 1969

Palladius

Prosper of Aquitaine records that in 431 Pope Celestine sent one Palladius, a deacon from Auxerre, to 'Scottos' to be their first bishop. The authenticity of this record can scarcely be challenged and there are traces, literary and archaeological, of this Palladius landing near Wicklow and founding three churches in the district. There is mention of his having given up his mission because of strong local opposition, and at least two of the relevant chronicles state that he sailed on to the land of the Picts (or, in another version, the Britons) where eventually he died in the Mearns, at Fordoun. An alternative tradition claimed that illness seized him within a year of landing in Ireland and he was dead by 432, a year later. This is quite possible, for in those days plague and other epidemics struck swiftly and with terrible effect, but in the case of Palladius this sudden demise is not convincing for it fits too neatly into the pattern which tradition desired. In 432 the Pope was supposed to dispatch a second missionary to Ireland to take the place of Palladius who, for whatever reason, had within the year disappeared. Room had to be made for Patrick.

The alternative account from other sources seems more likely—that Palladius crossed the channel to Alba and, living on, evangelised lands north of the Tay. There are some difficulties in this view. At that date Scotti almost certainly meant Irish people. If he found his reception in Wicklow too negative, surely he could have persevered for longer than a year before he fled north. In spite of the lack of supporting evidence perhaps the most likely reason was illness which made his proposed vigorous campaign in Ireland impossible but did not entirely prevent working quietly in Scotland until he died, leaving the glory of being Ireland's pioneer saint to the second choice, Patrick.

If we are right in thinking that Palladius spent his last years evangelising in Scotland it would account for the many local place-names and the tradition that he died in Pictish country. At Fordoun today, we find it known as 'Paldy parish' with a 'Paldy Well' and a 'Paldy Fair'. Further away, Aberfeldy is really 'Aberpaldy'. Canon Meissner, convinced that St 'Paldy' came to work in Scotland, believed he could trace his movements northwards from Ayrshire. He believed that the three churches he founded were not in Ireland but Scotland. The name of the third church, previously thought of as near Wicklow, Meissner placed at the village of Airth—its name in the Gaelic 'Domnach Airte' indicates 'The Lord's house in the high field'. Personally I believe there is much truth in Meissner's thesis, but I would not put the place south of the Forth at Airth, but with some confidence at what is today Logie Airte. Here Stirling university campus is situated, hard by an ancient kirk on a typically Celtic-type site and right at the foot of the last hill in the line of the Ochils, Dumyat.

We are told that in these parts Palladius lost two of his followers, Sylvester and Solinus (or Salonius) and at romantic moments one can imagine that their dust may still lie in this ancient graveyard. If this view of Palladius's mission be accepted it explains why he did little more than touch Irish soil as he sailed north and it accounts for the many closely-clustered 'Paldy' place-names in the Mearns.

To complete the picture, however, we must mention the views of one scholar, Dr A. B. Scott, who suggested that these references refer not to the Palladius sent over by the Pope but to an entirely different figure, one Pauldoc or Paul Hen—Paul the Aged—who was said to have worked with and encouraged David of Wales and in many ways brought together the British and Pictish Churches.

To return to place-names, in Glen Lyon is the waterfall 'Eas Phaldoc', while also on the Lyon is 'Ruighe Phaldoc', 'Paldy's sheiling'. At Dunning is St Paldoc's Lynn.

The festival of Palladius, be he the deacon sent by the Pope or the simple Celtic missioner, is 7 July.

D. H. Farmer, *Oxford Dictionary of Saints*, 1978
A. B. Scott, *The Pictish Nation*, 1918

PαꞱRICK It is true to say that the patron saint of Ireland has formed the subject of more learned controversy than all the other Celtic saints put together. A week after Dr Binchy published his great critique on 'The Saint and his Biographers' in *Studia Hibernica,* a Dublin bookseller picked up a copy of the new work and, flinging it across the counter to me, exclaimed, 'That solves the Patrician question for good; that's the last word and we can live in peace now.' But, of course, the bookseller was wrong. Irishmen were not to be done out of one of their favourite controversies so easily. Learned as

Binchy's work was, within a few months scholars were pulling it to pieces, and now twenty years later the debate continues.

Unlike the Scottish Ninian, who remains a shadowy, almost mythical figure, Patrick, in spite of having a legend built round him and the devotion of a nation behind him, is without any doubt, historical. In his *Confessio* and *Epistola* he has left two undoubtedly genuine writings and, once we have penetrated his obscure and sometimes ungrammatical language, we find a very human figure, who speaks to us in almost contemporary accents.

Patrick was a Briton, born on this side of the Irish Sea. As he tells us his father was a Roman civic official, he must have been brought up near a town where such an official might be found. We also know that this man, Calpornius, was a deacon of the Christian Church, although, like many other lads from Christian homes, Patrick confesses that he himself was not drawn to religion and suggests he remained a pagan. He tells us that the family home—perhaps just their villa or country farm—was at a place called Bannavem Taburniae, which remark has sent generations of scholars hunting for a place of this name, from Gaul to Dumbarton and from Cumbria to south Wales. Often suggested was Dumbarton, then called Alcluid, capital of the Strathclyde kingdom of the Britons. There were reasons which made this choice unlikely. A better suggestion was Caerwent in South Wales, an important Roman civil town. Clanaventa, now Maryport in Cumbria was, some thought, a corruption of Bannaventa and it had important Roman remains nearby. Scholars' preference today has moved to suggest places on or near Hadrian's Wall, and the Irthing valley would fit well with the picture of a band of raiders attacking an isolated farm and kidnapping members of the family. In his exhaustive work *Christianity in Roman Britain,* Thomas suggests 'the Greenhead Pass between the upper North Tyne at Haltwhistle and the upper gorge of the river Irthing' . . . a Romano-British estate of highland zone character, perhaps on the south side of the Irthing between Birdoswald and Lanercost.'

We see Patrick next as a slave under a heathen master, Miliuc either at the traditional spot, the hill Slemish in Ulster, or away in the west at Killala. During his captivity he had been converted to no conventional kind of faith. His *Confessio* is a document of burning evangelical zeal such as we might expect from a modern Salvation Army major. The saint does not claim to have the full support of the Church authorities—few such outspoken and fiery characters as Patrick have enjoyed a friction-free career. Prominent Churchmen, it seems, managed to dig up details of some unspecified doubtful incident from Patrick's past and used it against him.

This is, incidentally, one of the passages which show us that there were Christians and a Christian Church in Ireland before Patrick began his mission. It is also a suitable point to enquire where the mission took place and how extensive it was. Every parish in Ireland cherishes traditions of a visit from the great saint, and while a number of such claims are genuine and supported by early records, others stretch back no further than the Middle Ages.

If Patrick was a Briton taken to Irish captivity from Cumbria we would expect the traditions to be most numerous and most reliable in Ulster, especially in parts facing the Scottish coast. This is exactly what we do find. Not only are traditions about the saint more plentiful around that part, they also sound more authentic and primitive. Because of this, some Patrician students believe these may be the only authentic traditions and that Patrick the Briton never penetrated much further than a few miles from his original missionary centre at Sabhull (Saul) in County Down. The later accounts of his life, if we hold this view, belong not to Patrick the Briton but to a later missionary, perhaps of the same name, who has become confused with him and whom scholars have called the Second Patrick. We need not enquire here further into a second Patrick (who may have become entangled in the story of Palladius) but we must ask where our Patrick went when he escaped from Miliuc.

From some references in the *Confessio* and elsewhere, it was for long accepted by scholars that the captors left Patrick in Gaul and that he spent some years either with the celebrated Bishop Germanus at Auxerre or in the island monastery of Lerins on the Mediterranean coast, perhaps in both places. It is generally agreed that before or after his Gaulish studies he revisited his home in Britain. It is unlikely, however, that he studied in Gaul for any length of time. If he did so he must have been a particularly dull learner, for his Latin, while it has Gaulish traces, is elementary and full of grammatical errors. We suggest that he spent that period at home in Britain before the urgent inner call to Christ's service compelled him to cross the sea once again and begin missionary work in the little barn (Sabhull) whose successor may be seen beside Strangford Lough today.

What memories or traces of this great saint do we have today on this side of the channel? There is no sure evidence that he ever found time away from his chosen missionary work in Ireland to preach either in Scotland or England, yet both shores of the Solway have a great number of places bearing the saint's name in one form or another. In Dumfries and Galloway no less than four parishes look to him as patron—Kirkpatrick-Durham, Irongray, Juxta and Fleming. Across in Cumbria, dedications to Patrick include Aspatria, Patterdale, Bampton-Patrick, Preston-Patrick and Ousby. There are numerous dedications around Dumbarton, especially the districts of Old and New Kilpatrick. The farm Succoth in the same area may possibly derive from the saint's youthful name Sucat. Dalserf and Dalziel both remember Patrick and there is a Temple Patrick on Tiree and a Kilpatrick on Arran. The Church of Scotland today has six churches bearing his name.

St Patrick's day is 17 March.

D. A. Binchy, *Patrick and His Biographers*, Studia Hibernica No 2, 1962

R. P. C. Hanson, *St Patrick*, 1968

A. Marsh, *Saint Patrick and His Writings*, 1966

 PETER One of the most notable points concerning this saint is the fact that, while in England dedication of churches and parishes to him are almost too many to number, those in Scotland (apart from those of recent date) are very few. Reasons for this are two-fold. Firstly, the Celtic Churches, as developed among the Welsh, Picts, Britons and Gaidheals, did not dedicate churches to individuals but simply named them after the founders, or if they were already deceased, after the 'annat', the parent church from which they had sprung. Secondly, it seems true that eastern branches of the Church regarded St John of Ephesus with much the same degree of veneration as the western Church regarded St Peter, and when the practice of dedicating became usual, it was to John, or, even more usual, simply to a local respected missionary that the dedication was made.

The first group of Petrine dedications in Scotland can be traced to the arrival of Curitan (or Boniface) on the north shore of the Tay bearing a reply from the abbot of Jarrow to an enquiry from King Nechtan of the Picts as to correct ecclestical usages, including the type of tonsure and the dates of festivals. Nechtan had for some time been unsure of the validity of the customs of the Church in his dominions and was inclining toward the Roman practices which were gradually being adopted throughout western Christendom.

Curitan, an Irish Celtic priest, bore a long reply from Abbot Ceolfrid to the king at Scone. Nechtan had requested help to build a church 'after the style of the Romans' in Pictland. Restenneth priory is today taken to be this building. The lower courses of its tower are compatible in date and style, and Bede himself says that the Anglians sent masons to help to build 'after the Roman style'.

This church, standing in its fields quietly apart from the noisy bustle of Forfar, may well be the oldest example of ecclesiastical architecture in Scotland. Restenneth and all the churches built by the Anglian mission as it moved northwards were dedicated to Peter, the chief apostle. Local 'Celtic' dedications were viewed with some suspicion, and as the practice of dedicating buildings became general, the preference was for one of the apostolic band or, more often later, for the Virgin or the Angels. Where the old local saint was still held in great respect, the local name was often appended or prefixed to the major figure. As if by some perverse trait, some places clung to the old familiar saint and neglected to use the new name. We still find St Peter's at Invergowrie being called Kilcurdie, and another Kilcurdie at Rosemarkie should properly be St Peter's.

Both Roman Catholic and Scottish Episcopal Churches in modern times have paid respect to the old Celtic missionaries and accepted dedications to them almost as often as to the apostles. The Church of Scotland also has a large number of modern Petrine dedications.

Peter's festival is 29 June.

D. H. Farmer, *Oxford Dictionary of Saints*, 1978
A. B. Scott, *The Pictish Nation*, 1918

QUIVOX Formerly this saint (also called Kevoca and Mochaemhog) was taken to be a woman and commemorated under the name of St Kevoca the Virgin. The scholars Colgan and Lanigan treated him as feminine and a fictitious biography was ascribed to him. Reeves and Forbes finally showed the name to be simply a variant of Caemhog prefixed by the honorific 'mo'.

Of this seventh-century Connaught Christian almost nothing is known except that his father, Beoanus, was famed for craftsmanship and assisted St Ita in the building of her monastery. His mediaeval 'vita' is no more than a collection of pointless miracles. There is a tradition that Quivox worked in south-west Scotland, especially around Ayr, where he is remembered in the parish of St Quivox. At Eaglesham there is a Kevoch burn. Trained under St Ita and then at Bangor under Comgall, he is credited with founding the monastery of Liathmor, and is said to have died in 669.

His festival is 24 February.

A. P. Forbes, *Kalendars of Scottish Saints,* 1872

Regulus, or Rule, was probably one of the

very early Celtic missionaries in Fife who had his desertum in one of the caves on the shore near the site where later the great St Andrews cathedral would arise. A fourth-century date sometimes claimed for him would be a good deal too early even on this view of his life.

Various versions of his part in the transfer of St Andrew's relics to Kilrymont are hopelessly confused and should be discounted. These were probably given or sold to the town of St Andrews by Bishop Acca of Hexham. The story of the ship bearing the sacred bones being wrecked off the Fife coast may be discounted: the legends were politically contrived to boost the claims of the new see. The almost unknown Regulus was given a prominent part in the story, while the historical St Kenneth was played down although he probably had a major part in the early days of Kilrymont.

None of this, however, helps us to explain the great tower at St Andrews which bears Regulus's name and stands, a prominent puzzle for historians, so near the cathedral. It pre-dates the cathedral, but not by many years and its purpose is still debatable. It was quarried from remarkably good stone, found near at hand, and is in noticeably better condition than the later stone of the cathedral.

His festival is **17 October or 30 March.**

R. Kirk, *St Andrews,* 1954

G. A. F. Knight, *Archaeological Light on the Early Christianising of Scotland,* 1933

RONAN

RONAN We really know nothing of the life or work of Ronan of Innerleithen except that Walter Scott threw his magic mantle round him and so immortalised him and distinguished him for ever from the several other missionaries of the same name. At the synod of Whitby Bede tells us of a Ronan who was most zealous for the Roman Easter. It is possible but not probable that this was Sir Walter's Ronan.

A Ronan is remembered at several sites on Iona but nothing is known of him. Bishop Forbes identifies the Innerleithen Ronan with one at Kilmaronan in Lennox and this is probably the best guess, although questioned by Farmer. At the Well in Innerleithen annual festivities are still held. Knight makes him abbot of Kingarth, and a friend of St Modan.

His festival is 7 February or 1 June.

A. P. Forbes, *Kalendars of Scottish Saints*, 1872
G. A. F. Knight, *Archaeological Light on the Early Christianising of Scotland*, 1933

ROQUE

ROQUE (or Roche) left his home at Montpelier in the south of France about the middle of the fourteenth century and went on pilgrimage to Rome. On the way, however, he encountered a wave of the bubonic plague which had struck severely at the towns and villages of north Italy, and he turned his attention to nursing and caring for the stricken victims of this foul and fatal disease. How long he spent on this remedial work we do not know but in the end he contracted the disease himself and lay dying in a lonely place when he was rescued through the action of a dog which brought his master to the place through his barking and agitation.

In statues and paintings the dog is usually seen at the saint's side while he himself is pointing to a plague boil on his left thigh; death ensued if the boils did not burst and the legend claims the intervention of an angel who visited Roque and punctured the boil.

The Belgian scholar-monks in their great Bollandist chronicle of the lives of the saints accept the account of Roque's life only as far as the above, but popular traditions in France and Italy complete the story. After long wanderings during which he had been forgotten in his home town, the saint wandered back to Montpelier in dire poverty and emaciated by disease and hunger. Unrecognised, he was arrested by the town authorities and lodged in a verminous cell. Neglected in this way he died. The only food that he had during his imprisonment was brought to him by a stray mongrel dog. Only on the examination of his body after his death were documents found on it which revealed that he was Roque, nephew of the governor of the city.

He became a popular saint as he was considered to give protection from plague, and his chapels were places of refuge for the stricken. They were usually situated well outside the towns in isolation from other dwellings.

For long his spine was exhibited at Antwerp while Arles and Venice both claimed to have his relics. A litany lists his excellencies:

> St. Roch, lily of chastity, rose of charity, prodigy of humility,
> Marvel of resignation, visited by angels, joyful in imprisonment,
> Mirror of patience, model of pilgrims, health of the sick,
> Patron of pestilences, hope of the unhappy, preserver of public health,
> Pearl of affliction—
> From pestilence, cholera, typhus, deliver us.

Roque had at least five Scottish chapels in the Middle Ages. In Edinburgh the part of the Boroughmuir near Whitehouse Loan was the site of the chapel and cemetery for plague victims and a century ago, before the neighbourhood became built up, bones were still being dug up. There were considerable remains of the building until, in the middle years of last century, the proprietor ordered it all to be cleared. Workmen were reluctant to undertake the work and when, in the course of demolition, the scaffolding collapsed and some workers were killed, it was taken as indication of the saint's displeasure at desecration of his altar. This is the chapel mentioned by Scott in *Marmion* when he makes the hero look down from Blackford Hill over the Boroughmuir and the Sciennes. In *The Monarchie,* Lyndsay writes of the saint's image:

Sanct Roche, weill seisit, men may see
Ane byill new brokin on his thie.

And later:

Sum to St Roche with diligence
to saif thaim from the pestilence.

King James IV visited the chapel on the saint's day in 1507. In Dundee St Roque's chapel was situated outside the mediaeval city to the east of the Cowgate Port. A lane called after the saint existed until recent demolition cleared the area.

In Glasgow the saint's name has been altered to St Rollox, and the district where the chapel had stood took the title which last century became famous among engineers for its great locomotive building works. By 1736 the chapel had disappeared but there was still evidence of the cemetery.

In Paisley St Roque's chapel had a two-acre cemetery attached. In Stirling the chapel stood near the old bridge over the river. It will be noted that in each case the chapels were well away from town buildings, and all had large cemeteries.

The saint's festival is 16 August.

S. Baring-Gould and J. Fisher, *Lives of the British Saints,* 1913

J. Grant, *Old and New Edinburgh,* 1883

J. M. Mackinlay, *Ancient Church Dedications in Scotland,* Vol 2, 1914

SERF If you are among those to whom 'apostolic succession' means proving an unbroken link of ministry down from the apostles, then the date of Serf is of great importance, for the validity of the orders of many others depends on succession through this saint. This is perhaps why his dates have been a subject of great controversy.

It is generally accepted that Palladius was consecrated by Pope Celestine; tradition affirms that Palladius ordained Serf, who in turn ordained Kentigern (Mungo) at Culross and through him the whole stock of Celtic missionaries became regularised. So goes one line of argument, but to make it possible or even plausible you have to do a lot of juggling with dates, so we find the Bollandist scholars postulating two Serfs, if not three. If he was old enough to be ordained by Palladius, young enough to be at Culross when Kentigern was washed up on the shore but was also, as some say, contemporary with Adamnan, then he had a life-span of about three centuries.

If we take a mean between the extremes and geographically, for the moment, place Serf around the Ochil Hills, we may accept that one of his preaching centres was at Logie Airte, the little community at the foot of the last hill of the Ochils, Dumyat. This links up with what is suggested in the note on Palladius and also with

the chronicler Wyntoun, in whose *Chronikil* we
see Serf in action at Logie:

> This haly man had a ram
> That he had fed wp off a lame
> And oysyd hym to folow aye
> Quhare-ewyre he passyd in hys way;
> A theffe this schepe in Athren stall
> And ete hym wp in pesis small.
>
> Bot sone he worthyd rede for schame
> The schepe thare bletyd in hys wame.

'Wame' of course means 'stomach'! Not far
along the foothills from 'Athren' is Tillicoultry,
where:

> In Twlycultry till a wiffe
> Twa swnnys he rasyd fra dede to lyff.

The next village along the foothills, Alva, has
St Serf's well, formerly in the glebe of the church
which is dedicated to him. It was recently built
over by a housing scheme, and the house above
it is reputed to be damp. This whole area is so
marked by Serf dedications that he has rightly
been termed 'the apostle of the Ochils'. One
mediaeval narrative which credits him with
being 'the apostle of the Orkneys' had obviously
confused the two words. In Dunning, where later
he is said to have died:

> in Dovyn off his devotyoune
> And prayers, he slewe a fell dragowne;
> Qhare he wes slayne, that plas wes ay
> The dragownys den cald to this day.

So tenacious is the legend that if you ask for
Dragoden, or Dragon's Den today the local folk
will lead you to the place, although it seemed to
us to be the village dump. The very ancient
church of Dunning, of great architectural interest,
has just been vacated by the Church of Scotland
in favour of a nineteenth-century edifice, but
fortunately it will be preserved.

Serf's old bridge, deep in the Glendevon valley, is now submerged for a new water scheme. The motto of the former burgh of Auchtermuchty, 'Dum Sero Srero', is a pun on his name. The village of Dysart is so called from his retreat or *desertum* within the grounds of the present convent, while St Serf's island in Loch Leven contains the ruins of a later priory which supplanted earlier Culdee buildings with which the saint had some connection. Wyntoun, of the *Chronikil*, lived on this island, which probably gave him an added interest in Serf.

We have already mentioned many of the places connected with Serf. The parish of Fossaway is his, also Cardross, Newburn, Creich, Burntisland, Dalserf and St Serf's at Redgorton. At Tullibody his name is associated with St Kentigern.

In the Middle Ages popular but quite impossible legends arose making him a Jew, a descendant of a king of Canaan. The idea of any eastern connections may be instantly dismissed.

His festival is 1 July.

W. D. Simpson, *The Celtic Church in Scotland*, 1935
A. Wyntoun, *Orygynale Chronikil of Scotland*, 1872

*T*ARKIN In our note on St Donan we have told the dreadful story of the massacre on the island of Eigg of all fifty-two monks along with their abbot. It seems to be about as well authenticated as most traditions from that period can be, and indeed the names of the martyrs are alleged to have been preserved in almost contemporary martyrologies; through constant recopying, however, these have become so confused and corrupt as to be almost worthless and some scholars would regard the lists as fictitious. A. B. Scott, however, took the traditions seriously and traced the supposed routes of several of the Eigg missionaries as they planted settlements in the years before their martyrdom. Some of these quite probably enshrine authentic historical tradition. We dare not claim any of them to be reliable, but the most interesting and the most possible is the annual commemoration of St Tarkin in a holiday and fair in the small burgh of Fordyce, which until the educational reorganisation of recent years was famed throughout the whole north of Scotland for its academy. One of its great annual events was when the pupils, along with the whole community, remembered their patron, Tarkin—presumably the same saint as was remembered elsewhere in the north as Tarlorc, Tarloga or even Thalurgus.

Of the saint's life or his work before he rejoined his leader and returned to the western isle where they all suffered martyrdom in 618 we have not a single detail. We do know that Auchterless, further along the Firth, preserved many traditions of Saint Donan.

A. B. Scott, *The Pictish Nation*, 1918
W. D. Simpson, *The Celtic Church in Scotland*, 1935

Thomas

Thomas One might well ask why an English archbishop, even one as illustrious as Thomas à Becket, finds a place in a book about Scottish saints. The answer is, of course, that within eight years of Becket's murder, on the rash order of King Henry, his cult had spread so rapidly and so widely that King William of Scotland chose him as patron saint of his new abbey at the mouth of the Brothwick Burn, and declared that the grey-robed Tironensian monks, whom he brought up from Kelso to staff it, should not be dependent on the older abbey but be 'free of all submission and obedience to the parent house'.

The murder of Becket had been a personal tragedy for the Scottish king for he had in his schooldays been a frequent visitor at King Henry's court and had become a close friend of the future archbishop. He must have watched with dismay the estrangement between the king and Becket who resigned the important position of chancellor when he became bishop. Three years after Becket became archbishop William became king of Scotland. Three years after Henry had called on his knights to rid him of 'this troublesome priest' Becket was canonised, and his cult spread with astonishing rapidity. Within a few years in England, eighty churches counted him as patron. Meantime King William of Scotland had been captured by the English at the battle of Alnwick. On his release from prison in Normandy, when his boat landed at the mouth of the Brothwick Burn, he founded Arbroath abbey and heaped gifts and endowments on it until it had in its patronage no less than two dozen parishes, countless other privileges and the peculiar treasure of the historic Brecbennoch of St Columba.

Thomas's festival is 29 December.

Vigean or Fechin

Vigeanus is simply a Latinisation of the Irish Fechin and it is under the latter title that the saint is known in his native Ireland. In the *Felire of Oengus* there is a story which, if it were true, would in no way be to his credit. During a time of scarcity, it was said, it was agreed at an assembly of clergy and laity to set limits on the amount of land which might be owned by any one person and the clergy were ordered to pray that the number of the 'lower orders' might be reduced by pestilence to leave more food for the others. Vigean, who voted for this motion himself, died in the great visitation of the yellow plague, probably in 664.

It may be hoped that this story is as wide of the facts as many of the miracles in the three extant 'lives' of our saint. Vigean was a friend of the saints Ultan and Ronan, and his life relates that the three all prayed for blessings on Ireland: Vigean that there should never be famine, Ultan that there should never be plague, and Ronan that she should never be invaded. Historically it would seem that these prayers of the saints did not avail much, for the country has from time to time suffered from all three.

At Fore in West Meath, there are still interesting, if fragmentary, remains going back to the saint's time. He had also foundations at Cong and Bellysadare but of his work in Scotland there are only place-names, which might arise from a

233

later cultus. O'Hanlon, who devotes a chapter to his work in Ireland, denies that Vigean ever worked in Scotland. A. B. Scott, with very little authority, sets him in the framework of the Whithorn mission. Knight, pointing to several Angus place-names and the typically Celtic site of St Vigean's kirk near Arbroath, almost persuades us that Vigean did work in the district. As Fechin he is remembered in Ecclefechan and perhaps at Torphichen. Watson suggested that Lesmahagow is really Lios-mo-fhegu or fhecu. St Vigean's itself now possesses a museum with various Pictish stones.

'Fechin' can signify in Gaelic a 'raven' and the *Felire of Oengus* claims his mother gave him this name when she found him chewing a bone which had dropped out of a nest. The Irish life of the saint pays him a remarkable tribute:

> prayerful, skilful, holy-worded ... possessed of illuminated books, a man of a bright summery life ... fair-worded Fechin of Fore.

His festival is 20 January.

A. P. Forbes, *Kalendars of Scottish Saints*, 1872

G. A. F. Knight, *Archaeological Light on the Early Christianising of Scotland*, 1933

D. Pochin Mould, *The Irish Saints*, 1964

Wilfred Born in Northumbria in 633 and educated at Lindisfarne, Wilfred showed, even in early years, little satisfaction with the Celtic Christian customs he saw round him and, encouraged by Queen Enfleda and some monks, he went to Canterbury and on to Rome where he studied. Returning to England by way of Gaul he was invited by King Aldfrith to become abbot of Ripon, where he introduced Roman customs and the Benedictine Rule. Already competent in ecclesiastical stratagem, he managed to secure the favour of the King Egfrith and Queen Etheldreda.

Wilfred raised his own prestige and that of other prelates, and kept great state. His church at Hexham was reckoned to be finest north of the Alps. He is most often portrayed as an early example of the clever, proud and far from humble ecclesiastic and this picture seems fairly true. He is usually met in history books proclaiming the case in favour of Roman usages at the famous synod of Whitby in 663–4. If we dismiss the simplification that at Whitby clerics got excited about the simple chronology of church festivals, and try to probe deeper, we cannot do better than to read the analysis made by the German scholar Heinrich Zimmer of the real differences between Celtic and Roman usages. Efficiency, discipline, orderliness, uniformity, careful counting of the cost of every step the Church made and conformity to a great extent with the accepted standards and practices of the wider world—against this picture of the factors inspiring Roman usage were ranged the Celtic traditions of wide local differences and personal choice, little concern with efficiency as such, looser discipline and too great willingness to accept deviations from the mean.

To pass to an acute modern commentator on Whitby and on Wilfred, we look at Henry Mayr-Harting: 'There is no other evidence of friction between adherents of the Roman and Ionan Easters until three years or so before the synod; Aidan was held in universal esteem by everyone, including the archbishop of Canterbury.'

What Mayr-Harting is saying is that the argument, in the context of that synod, was a great mistake largely engineered by the chief actor, Wilfred. Mayr-Harting, of course, recognises fully the importance of the date of Easter, but it could probably have been settled more quietly and with consideration for the good of the Church with patience on both sides. Of the final judgement at Whitby, Mayr-Harting quotes the words of the contemporary music-master monk, Edius Stephanus, that King Oswy gave his judgement 'with a smile'.

Wilfred's festival is 12 October.

D. H. Farmer, *Oxford Dictionary of Saints*, 1978
H. Mayr-Harting, *The Coming of Christianity*, 1972

Index

of Scottish counties and cities where there is some evidence that the cult of individual saints was observed.

Inverness   Adamnan, Columba, Comgall, Kenneth, Moluag

Kincardine   Colm, Cyrus, John the Evangelist, Laurence, Marnock, Palladius

Kinross   Martin, Ninian, Serf

Kirkcudbright   Cuthbert, John the Baptist, Michael

Lanark   Constantine, Kentigern, Oswald

Midlothian   Margaret, Michael

Moray   Gerardine, Giles, Maelrubha, Margaret, John Ogilvie

Orkney   Christopher, Magnus, Olaf

Peebles   Bega, Gordian, Kentigern, Llolan, Ronan

Perth   Adamnan, Aidan, Blane, Catan, Conan, Fillan, Fintan Munnu, George, John the Baptist, Kentigern, Macdonald Maidens, Michael, Triduana

Renfrew   Convall, Mirren

Ross and Cromarty   Comgan, Curitan, Duthac, Kentigerna, Maelrubha, Peter, Ronan

Roxburgh   Boisil, Cuthbert, Kentigern

Selkirk   Bega, Kentigern

Shetland Isles   Magnus, Olaf

Stirling   Kenneth, Kentigerna, Llolan, Palladius

Sutherland   John the Evangelist

Western Isles   Baithene, Brendan, Bride, Christopher, Colmanella, Columba, Comgall, Donan, John the Evangelist, Kenneth, Modwenna, Moluag

Wigtown   Bride, Colm, Comgan, Donan, Finian, John the Evangelist, Katherine of Alexandria, Malachy, Martin, Medan, Michael, Modwenna, Ninian, Patrick

Furth of Scotland

Cumbria   Andrew, Bega, Cuthbert, Herbert, Kentigern, Martin, Ninian, Oswald, Patrick

Northumbria   Aidan, Colman, Cuthbert, Ebba, Godric, Hilda, Oswald